tinkered
treasures

tinkered
treasures

more than 35 easy-to-make projects
to bring charm to the everyday

Elyse Major

CICO BOOKS
LONDON NEW YORK

To my guys, with love.

Published in 2013 by CICO Books
An imprint of Ryland Peters & Small
519 Broadway, 5th Floor,
New York NY 10012
20–21 Jockey's Fields,
London WC1R 4BW

www.cicobooks.com

10 9 8 7 6 5 4 3 2 1

A CIP catalog record for this book
is available from the Library of
Congress and the British Library.

ISBN: 978-1-908862-56-3

Printed in China

Editor: Marie Clayton
Designer: Lucy Parissi
Photographer: Holly Jolliffe
Stylist: Sophie Martell
Illustrator: Qian Wu

contents

Foreword

As an editor for several home decorating magazines, I routinely peruse the blog world in search of out-of-the-ordinary interiors and fabulous artists. One very lucky day I found Tinkered Treasures, Elyse Major's blog, which features both her house and some of her crafts. That chance encounter led to a photoshoot at her cottage, our ongoing friendship, and this lovely book, aptly named after her much-acclaimed blog.

Upon entering Elyse's darling cottage I was instantly smitten, seduced, and fascinated by the way she decorates, and the numerous little treasures she makes—each room was even more endearing than the next and each showcased several of her whimsical and captivating creations.

Elyse's "tinkering" began in childhood when she first fell under the spell of soft paint colors, pretty papers and fabrics, glue sticks, and all manner of simple embellishments. Her affection for creating loveliness grew with every passing year and shaped her career path—she started out as an arts and crafts instructor, then further honed her skills in advertising and public relations, followed by becoming a regular contributor to home and decor magazines and, now, author.

More often than not, recycling equates with clever or functional but rarely with pretty and delightful. Yet, that's exactly what *Tinkered Treasures* accomplishes. Elyse's artful designs reflect her sensibility in transforming the most prosaic objects into beautiful and useful items. Under her fairy-like fingers plain glass jars are reborn into enchanting painted containers with floral decoupage appliqués, little sprites spring from old spools, dolls from clothespins, and magnets take on the appearance of luscious confections, to name but a few. Even if you are a craft novice you will love spending time with this charming book in which personal creativity is not only encouraged, but celebrated. The possibilities are as exciting as they are limitless. Aside from their obvious singular beauty, the appeal of the numerous inspiring projects lies in their simplicity, affordability, versatility, and usefulness. Recycling never looked so glorious!

Many people just dream of seeing their ideas become reality. Very few have the determination, vision, and passion to make it happen. Elyse's *Tinkered Treasures* is proof positive that when dreamers become creators, magic happens.

FIFI O'NEILL
Romantic Prairie Style

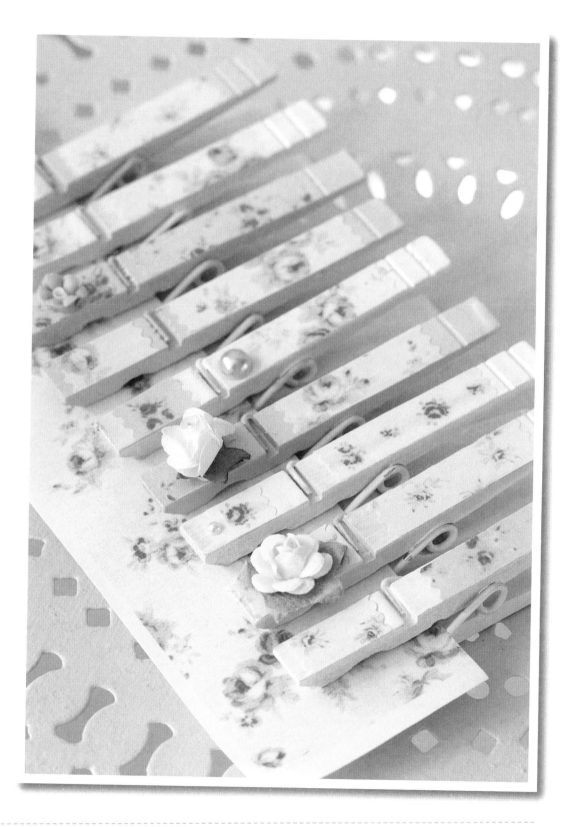

Introduction

In the fairy tale of Rumplestiltskin, a small troll has the ability to turn straw into gold. *Tinkered Treasures* will empower you to do similar acts of enchantment by coaching you to convert commonplace items into pretty things for your home, office, and gift giving. It all begins with looking at everyday objects in new ways.

I affectionately refer to such transformations as "tinkering" because the word describes working with things in an unskilled or experimental manner. Tinkering is not constructing: it's embellishing, repurposing, altering. Tinkering is about leaving behind any worries of perfection and appreciating the flaws. Tinkering is about making a little time to add playful details to your life.

Each craft project in this book is meant for skill level easy! Measuring often gives way to estimating and many of the simple techniques are repeated from project to project. The book will show how to tinker inconspicuous sundries, supplies, recyclables, and bits and bobs into fanciful keepsakes. It is recommended that you keep almost every pretty scrap, because some projects will make use of even the smallest piece of paper or remnant of fabric.

If you are new to crafting have no fear because, after a comprehensive Getting Started section, simple step-by-step instructions are provided for each project. Many projects can be made by children, with adult assistance. The projects in this book are all very adaptable to conceal or revel in imperfections—whichever suits you—and, with simple color or pattern changes, the ideas presented are easily translated to any style preference, season, or holiday.

"One of the secrets of a happy life is continuous small treats."
IRIS MURDOCH

Tinkering does not require much time or space. Most projects can be completed rather quickly, or in small stages that are easy to pause and resume. Find any pleasant spot where you can be comfortable and, with a sheet of wax paper to protect the surface and a few tools, you are ready to make a glorious mess.

Tinkering is playing, because isn't life a little more fun when we surround ourselves with things that make us smile? I hope you enjoy making these projects and discover the rewarding bliss of creativity.

GETTING STARTED

Once you begin to tinker, you might surprise yourself by suddenly scrutinizing all kinds of common things to determine their treasure potential. Start a collection almost instantly simply by rifling through a junk drawer or sifting through your stack of recyclables. As for tools, many tried-and-true implements used in this book are actually school supplies, such as a glue stick and a sharp pair of scissors. Rest assured that the techniques provided are just as uncomplicated. Tinkering is a no-pressure endeavor.

Materials

Each project in this book calls for items that have been divided into two groups: Materials and Tools. The Materials list comprises workaday items collected from around the house—things such as clothespins, jars, and matchboxes—plus special purchases like gems, paper roses, and ribbon. A Tinker Tip is sometimes provided as a helpful recommendation; Fancy This offers additional project uses or variations.

I keep a few grocery bags in my basement, each filled with sorted, emptied cans and jars, produce baskets and bottles—their labels removed, rinsed well, and dried—ready for decorating. Many objects are interesting on their own so imagine what a little paint, paper, and embellishing can do! Be on the lookout for items that are relatively sturdy in structure and that can be used in different ways.

Following is a list of favorite materials and tools with which to work. Seemingly small adornments, trusty supplies, and proven methods will bestow enjoyment and charm to any project. For purchasing information, please see Suppliers on page 126.

Treasure: Paper cupcake liners, matchboxes, clothespins, jars, cans, paper tubes, small boxes, lunch bags, paper-paint chips, plastic CD cases, unused toothpicks, paper doilies, bottle caps, wooden spools, egg cartons, paper cups, paper napkins, containers from farmers' markets.

Adhesive gems: Like their jewelry-making "cousins," cabochons, these gems made for scrapbooking have flat backs but, unlike "cabs," adhesive gems require no glue. They are available in a range of sizes and a variety of finishes, from metal to pearl to rhinestone.

Baker's twine: Twisted strands of two colors make baker's twine a tasteful and nostalgic addition to projects that call for hanging or tying.

Embroidery floss: The low cost and a wide assortment of colors make this cotton thread a great choice for projects that require hanging or tying.

Fabric: The fabrics used in this book—either as-is or copied or scanned onto pretty paper (*see page 16*)—are all cotton quilting fabrics.

Glitter: Use the glitter you like best for projects. I tend to reach for fine glitter for its subtle glint. Medium glitter, often used for children's crafts, is low-cost and easy to find. When a project calls for complete coverage, opt for inexpensive medium or large, white or crystal glitter, available in plastic jars with a slot opening for easy pouring. For extra special accents try German glass glitter, made from shards of colored glass silver-coated for added shine, which will develop a patina over time; this glitter is not recommended for use with children.

Millinery forget-me-nots: Flocked bunches of dainty flowers and blossoms, generally found in 12 floral sprigs on paper-wrapped wire stems, add sweetness to any project. Seek these vintage items in specialty or old craft or fabric stores, or from online retailers.

Paper fasteners, brads, or split pins: These stationery-store staples—once found only in brass—have become a scrapbooking accessory, offered in a plethora of designs. Use to hold things together by inserting the closed tines through a hole and then bending them open.

Paper roses: Small roses made of paper can be found twisted in wired clusters, or with adhesive backing. Use to add instant cottage charisma to any project.

Ribbon: When you find "ribbon" in a project list, the choice is yours, from grosgrain to satin, patterned or plain, wide or narrow. My favorite ribbon to work with is seam binding, for its pliability and soft sherbet shades. Like millinery forget-me-nots, seek this vintage item in specialty or old craft or fabric stores, or from online retailers.

Craft sticks & chenille sticks (pipe cleaners): Craft sticks can be purchased in packets at the craft store—or you can just save wooden ice-pop sticks, washing them well before use. Chenille sticks are also widely available and come in a range of colors.

Paint: When projects in this book call for paint, almost any type will do. You may use acrylic craft paint, which is available in a multitude of colors and varied finishes like satin or high-gloss, and is made for different uses such as applying to wood or metal. Another option is to visit your local paint retailer and

purchase tester-sized containers of interior latex in white base (7¾ fluid ounces/230 ml), tinted with your favorite color(s) selected from literally thousands of paint chips. You can even have paint color-matched to your favorite paper and/or fabric. Ask to have your tester pot mixed just as you would larger quantities. Use spray paint for covering intricate surfaces thoroughly or painting many pieces at once. Spray paint can be used on wood, metal, ceramic, and more. Be sure to follow the manufacturer's directions and use outdoors during calm, dry weather for best results.

TINKER TIP Pass on tinkering things that are not worth the effort. Some examples:
- cans that once contained chemicals
- anything with sharp edges
- something you might not be able to get perfectly clean and odor-free, like perhaps a tuna can or ice cream carton

Tools

The tools you need are so basic that you will almost certainly have some at home already. If not, they are readily available at craft stores and are generally inexpensive. With the more expensive items—such as decorative punches—buy good-quality versions as and when you need them, rather than purchasing random designs that you may not use.

Decoupage medium: This refers to products like Mod Podge®, an all-in-one glue, sealer, and finish.

Foam Brushes: Readily available on the cheap at craft and home improvement stores, foam brushes are perfect for applying decoupage medium and latex and craft paint. To clean them, rinse with warm water and squeeze until the water runs clear.

Glue: Most projects in this book call for white craft glue, which is pretty much interchangeable with school glue. When gluing paper, I find it best to use a glue stick because it does not dampen paper.

Paper plates: Sturdy, pliable, and recyclable, paper plates make nice palettes for paint. Use them when sprinkling glitter; they will not only contain mess but you can then roll and funnel them to return excess glitter to containers.

Scissors: For best results, use a sharp pair of scissors for cutting and trimming. When edges show in a project, consider using **Pattern-edge scissors**, which create wavy and scalloped patterns as they cut.

Pinking shears: These leave a nice zigzag pattern and are useful for cutting cloth and giving projects a homespun quality.

Paper punches: Hand-held hole punches are perfect for making round openings from tiny to small. For larger shapes, try a decorative punch featuring one of the following shapes: scalloped circles, flowers, hearts, or stars. Try an edge punch for making continuous lace and floral-like patterns.

Pencil: This is mostly used in the early stages of the project for marking cutting lines and drawing shapes. An ordinary Number 2 (HB) pencil is fine.

Ruler: A clear plastic ruler is the best option to use because it allows you to see through it and at whatever you are working on; choose a type that has a good range of measuring options. Do not use a plastic ruler to cut against, as the edge can be easily damaged and is then no longer accurate for measuring.

Permanent marker: A few projects use these for long-lasting drawing or lettering. They are easy to find in a range of colors in stationery or craft stores.

Painter's tape: This low-tack tape is designed to mask areas and stop paint spreading where it's not wanted while it is applied. Find it in home improvement stores.

Math compass: An ordinary school math compass is perfect for projects that call for making circles.

Clips: Some items may have to be held in place while the glue sets. Keep a few plastic clips—or clothespins—on hand for this.

Wax paper: Found in the market alongside parchment paper and foil, wax paper is my go-to for protecting a work area. Easy to tear off the roll in any size, wax paper is semi-translucent, so it is not dark and distracting. Wax paper is also moisture-proof, making it the perfect choice when working with glue and paint.

Making Pretty Paper & Pretty Labels

At the heart of most every project in this book is what I refer to as "pretty paper." I am drawn to displays of petite clusters of roses and blossoms on cotton in a palette of faded pastels but the truth is that as much as I adore fabric, the skills required for sewing—such as measuring and cutting precisely—frighten me away every time. Never able to find exactly what I wanted in paper at the craft store, I decided to create my own. Take color copies of your favorite prints and make beautiful projects using paper and glue rather than fabric and thread.

MATERIALS

Favorite fabrics (cotton quilting fabrics work best)

Printer paper, letter size (A4) multipurpose

Card stock (optional)

Standard 1 x 2⅝in. (2.5 x 6.5cm) mailing labels, white, 30 labels per sheet

TOOLS

Iron and ironing board

Scanner and color printer or color copier

1 Find beautiful fabrics that make your heart race. Begin by sorting through a stash of cotton fabric remnants, borrow fabric from a friend, or purchase small quantities like "fat quarter" bundles. Pieces do not need to be any larger than letter size paper and will not be damaged.

2 Using manufacturer-recommended settings, iron out any creases. Determine if you will scan fabrics at home or take to a copy center to print in color. If making pretty labels, you will need to scan fabrics.

3 Place one fabric at a time neatly on the glass of a scanner or copier, avoiding any folds. Print as-is or experiment with adjusting settings to reduce or enlarge, lighten or darken, heighten or lower contrast. A single piece of fabric can look vastly different after print settings have been changed.

4 Use standard paper for most projects but also copy a small supply onto white or ivory cardstock for tinkering heavier-weight items like bookmarks. You now have an inventory of custom pretty paper for tinkering!

5 For pretty labels, scan the fabric making sure to prevent any folds. Experiment with adjusting settings until your image is how you want it to be: reduced or enlarged, darker or lighter, high or low contrast, or as-is.

6 Scanned images should be "Saved As" in a format that can be uploaded (Jpeg, for instance) into a label template. Does that sound too complicated? Photograph fabrics instead.

7 Upload the fabric images into a mailing label template. You may need to adjust the size of your image to fit in each label field.

8 Consider overlaying a text box that has "no fill" and "no outline" and type in words or phrases over the images.

9 Print the design on an adhesive mailing label sheet. You now have 30 pretty labels to use as you desire!

TINKER TIPS Make multiple copies of your very favorite fabrics as pretty paper to have handy for repeated use and for projects that require more than one sheet of paper.

Use scraps of pretty label in place of paper strips and glue for smaller projects that call for scraps, or substitute for tape.

Enlarge favorite motifs like rose clusters to use on projects such as the Treasure Box (*see page 26*) *or* Desk Tidy (*see page 60*).

Instead of fabric, copy wallpaper samples or patterned napkins.

FANCY THIS Coordinate projects to match rooms, fabric gifts, and more.

Trimming & Tearing Motifs

Numerous projects in this book call for cutting a motif or an image from paper. Choosing to cut challenging images, such as an intricate cluster of roses and their petals, can be arduous but with a bit of practice you'll be up for the challenge! If precision cutting is not for you, cut small squares or tear pieces to create collages on projects, or substitute cut images with stickers or decals.

1 Begin by cutting your chosen image within a tight square.

2 Next, get even closer by cutting straight lines from point to point followed by snipping away any triangles.

3 Finally it's time to drive! Hold paper with your non-dominant hand and slowly steer and turn the image while cutting with scissors in your dominant hand.

4 Tearing paper or fabric instead of cutting with scissors gives projects a slightly tattered quality. For fabric, use scissors to make a small snip at a suitable edge and then slowly tear in two.

5 For paper, tear into the desired sizes, taking care not to wrinkle the paper— unless you like wrinkles!

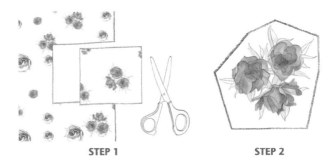

STEP 1   **STEP 2**

STEP 3

TINKER TIP If you accidentally snip off a small piece such as a leaf, simply reposition it on the main portion once glued onto the project surface.

Decoupage

To decoupage is to cut images or motifs from paper, stick them to something, and then seal with layers of finish. Avoid getting items wet after they have been decoupaged.

1 Trim an image from paper as described in Trimming Motifs (*see page 18*). Pour a small circle of decoupage medium onto a paper plate.

2 Lightly brush or stipple (make small dots of) decoupage medium to the back of your cut image or apply the glue stick, and gently position on project surface and press to fix in place.

3 Brush a light coat of decoupage medium over the image using a dry foam brush. Cover the entire top-surface to give a consistent finish all over.

STEP 2

STEP 3

4 Smooth any wrinkles gently with your fingers either after a few minutes or immediately using direct heat from a blow dryer.

5 Let dry and then continue to add coats of decoupage medium, allowing to dry in between coats until you have the finish you want.

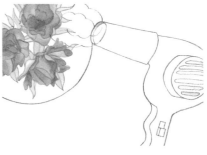

STEP 4

Using Glue

Large amounts of adhesive are not needed to get the job done and heavy applications slow down your project due to lengthy dry-time. Choosing the correct glue for the material is also key for good results.

1 Always make sure that you apply glue sparingly in thin lines or small dots.

2 My method of glue-stick application is to begin at the center of the paper and move away in all directions, as if drawing rays of sunshine.

3 For applying braid, run the glue stick lightly along the reverse of the braid. Be careful not to get glue on the front surface.

4 When applying very thin strokes of glue for glitter application, use a fine-point glue pen or dip a toothpick into glue.

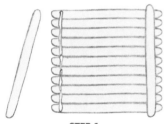

STEP 1

STEP 3

STEP 4

chapter 1
tinkering sundries

I suppose the roots of my tinkering can be traced back to childhood when I was instantly smitten with the technique of tinting small mounds of table salt with colored chalk, then pouring them color-by-color into shapely jars to showcase the soft-hued layers. It therefore seems especially fitting to begin this book with a section of projects based on small, miscellaneous things you might just have handy at home—perhaps some small matchboxes from a kitchen drawer, clothespins off the line, or emptied spools from the sewing tin. Smile, find a sunny spot, and prepare to render an assortment of humble nothings into wonderful somethings.

little drawers

Decorating small matchboxes is fun, fast, and easy because their diminutive size requires only scraps of material or time. These little drawers—which I refer to in French as Les Petits Tiroirs—are perfectly suited for presenting small gifts.

MATERIALS
Small matchboxes
Pretty paper (*see page 16*)
Gems, beads, or buttons
Embellishments such as
    millinery flowers
Lengths of ribbon

TOOLS
Ruler or paper cutter
Scissors
Pattern-edge scissors
    (optional)
Glue stick
Wax paper to protect
    work surface

FANCY THIS Personalize a selection of drawers with names and use as favors or place cards, or delight a houseguest by leaving one on their bed pillow at night.
   Another lovely idea is to create a set of 25 boxes for display as a Christmas Advent calendar!

1 Begin by emptying and safely disposing of the contents of your matchboxes. Cut your selected paper into two rectangles for each box: 2 x 4in. (5 x 10cm) for the outer cover and 1¼in. (3cm) by just under 2in. (5cm) to line the base of the drawer.

2 Trim the edges of the paper with pattern-edge scissors for extra detail. Cut an additional 2 x 1in. (5 x 3cm) from plain white paper to stick on top of each matchbox if you wish to keep any graphics on the outer sleeve from showing through the decorated paper.

3 Using the glue stick, lightly coat the outside of a matchbox with adhesive and then wrap the box with the large rectangle of paper, which should fit almost perfectly. Remove the inside "drawer" and lightly bend the matchbox to-and-fro to crease the folds in the paper. Trim off any excess as needed.

4 Lightly coat the inside bottom of the matchbox drawer with adhesive using the glue stick and place the smaller rectangle of paper down inside the drawer; gently rub to fix the paper in place.

5 Add a gem, bead or button to the drawer front to act as a faux pull (simply for show), if desired. Tie a ribbon around the box, tucking a few millinery flowers into the knot, or gluing on a small bead or paper rose. Repeat Steps 3–5 to complete the other matchboxes.

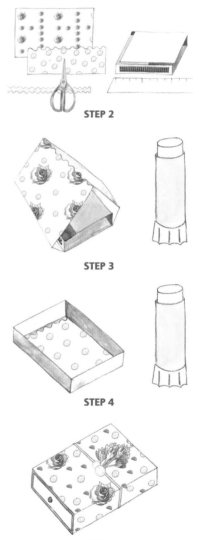

STEP 2

STEP 3

STEP 4

STEP 5

treasure box

A box built from craft sticks makes a charming treasure chest befitting a beach cottage; use to corral seaside finds or souvenirs. This summer camp pastime comes of age with a wash of color, a sweet image, and a sprinkle of glitter.

MATERIALS
58 or more craft sticks
Image on paper
Paint, latex or craft
Glitter
Small square of decorative fabric or felt

TOOLS
Craft glue
Foam brush
Paper plates for decoupage, paint palette, and glitter tray
Scissors
Decoupage medium
Glue pen
Wax paper to protect work surface

FANCY THIS Glue a pretty faux handle to the top of the lid—use a large bead or button, a paper flower, a seashell.

1 Neatly line 11 craft sticks side-by-side. Secure with two sticks glued lengthwise across the top and bottom, leaving a small margin at the tips. Set aside as your lid. Repeat to create the base.

2 Begin to build walls around the base as you would a log cabin, alternating between sides, using dots of craft glue to secure. Continue until the walls are about 8 sticks high, or the height you prefer. Once your box is complete, set aside to dry.

3 For a weathered appearance, apply paint using a dry foam brush. Paint each side of the box and lid but do not worry about even coverage. Apply as many coats as desired and leave to dry completely.

4 Carefully trim the image and apply a light coat of decoupage medium to the reverse. Gently press the image to the top of the lid, smoothing out bubbles or creases and pressing against any grooves. Brush over the image with a light coat of decoupage medium and let dry.

5 Add glitter one color at a time by applying light, fine strokes using a glue pen (or toothpick dipped in craft glue) to desired areas then sprinkling glitter over the lines of glue. Shake off excess glitter by gently tapping on the lid. Allow to dry.

6 Measure the base inside the box and cut a piece of fabric or felt to fit. Put a few dabs of craft glue on the reverse of the fabric and carefully place it inside the box.

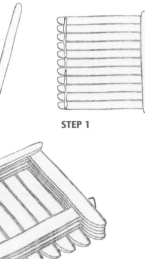

STEP 1

STEP 2

STEP 4

STEP 5

pretty clothespins

Reliable and sturdy, wooden clothespins have long been used to secure linens to lines and are available at the laundry aisle of most supermarkets. One pack will give you plenty to decorate, use, and share. Use your one-of-a-kind clip art to secure tags and keep sacks shut, or to post an indoor clothesline to display mittens, dish towels, Valentines, and more.

MATERIALS
Wooden clothespins, with springs
Pretty paper (*see page 16*)
Embellishments such as paper roses, gems, small buttons

TOOLS
2 bricks and 1 dowel rod to create a drying rack
Newspaper to protect outdoor work surface
Spray paint
Sand paper, optional
Scissors
Pattern-edge scissors, optional
Glue stick
Decoupage medium
Paper plate as a palette for decoupage medium
Foam brush
Craft glue
Wax paper to protect indoor work surface

1 Prepare an area outdoors for spray-painting: you need a flat surface on which to stand two bricks, about 12in. (30cm) apart—the bricks will serve as a perch for your dowel, as spray-painted clothespins drip-dry. Cover the area beneath with newspaper. Anchor the newspaper at each corner with rocks to prevent it from flapping in the breeze and sticking to wet paint.

2 Clip a row of clothespins to the dowel rod, leaving about a finger's width between each clothespin. Leave some of the dowel rod free at each end for handling and then perching atop the bricks.

3 Hold one end of the rod in one hand and the can of spray paint with your other hand. Rotate the rod of clothespins as you lightly spray with paint. Perch the rod, pick up by the other end and repeat. You may also spray while the rod is perched and stationary, but I find that rotating offers the best coverage.

4 Perch the rod of painted clothespins across the two bricks and allow to dry; there will be drips. If you wish, apply a second coat. Let dry completely (overnight). Peel off any dried drips and sand to a smooth finish, if desired.

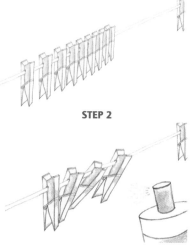

STEP 2

STEP 3

STEP 5

STEP 6

5 Gather scraps of paper for covering the two flat areas of each clothespin; pieces will need to be approximately ¾in. (2cm) long for the upper portion and about 2in. (5cm) for the bottom, with a width of about ⅜in. (9mm). Trim edges with pattern-edge scissors for extra detail. Use pre-cut strips or place approximately sized strips and then trim off the excess.

6 Dab the glue stick over the back of the paper, then place on the clothespin and smooth flat. Apply a light coat of decoupage medium, allow to dry, and then add another light coat. Let dry. Add further embellishments, if desired, using craft glue.

TINKER TIP Be sure to leave the end of each clothespin free of embellishments so that you do not hinder the ability to pinch it open.

FANCY THIS Keep tickets and photographs in sight by securing Pretty Clothespins to a wide, framed mirror using wood glue or a hot-glue gun. Display notices on the fridge by adding magnetic strips to the backs of the Pretty Clothespins.

clothespin dolls

View round-headed clothespins through the eyes of a toymaker and discover the makings of pocket-sized pals. Bear witness to personalities taking shape as you bend chenille-stick (pipe cleaner) arms, snip cupcake-wrapper skirts, and mark simple facial features. Plant finished dolls firmly in frosting to decorate cupcakes, hang from strings as ornaments, or create a coterie for display or play.

MATERIALS

One-piece wooden clothespin or "doll pin" with round top
Fused pearls (optional)
Pretty label (*see page 16*)
Seam binding
Cupcake liners
Ribbons
Chenille sticks (pipe cleaners)
Millinery flowers, gems
Wooden doll-pin stand

TOOLS

Clear nail polish
Fine-point permanent markers
Fine-line paint marker
Craft glue
Scissors
Pattern-edge scissors, optional
Small clips or elastics to hold pieces in place while drying

TINKER TIP Read all directions before you begin because steps 1–3 require time to dry.

1 Apply a light coat of clear nail polish to the head of the clothespin. This will prevent the ink from bleeding into the wood grain when you draw the face. Allow to dry.

2 Practice how you will draw the face and hair on paper first and, when ready, draw these onto the head of the clothespin. Use the permanent marker for all the facial features and the paint marker for the hair. Allow the paint marker to dry.

3 If the doll is to have a necklace, trim a string of fused pearls to fit around the neck. Add glue to the neck area, place the beads around the neck and clamp the ends together at the back of the head. Allow to dry.

4 For undergarments, use pattern-edge scissors to trim a strip of pretty label and place it around your doll at the top of the "legs" before dressing. Create a bodice by wrapping, trimming, and gluing a piece of seam binding around the doll pin on the upper body.

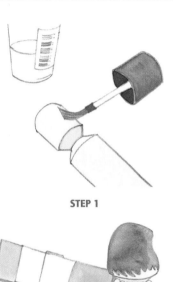

STEP 1

STEP 3

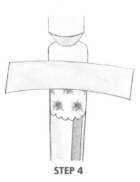

STEP 4

5 Fold a cupcake liner in half and make a small slit in the center at the fold. Open out and carefully slide onto the doll pin, adjusting to form a skirt. Fold the two outer thirds in so that they overlap at the doll pin's back.

6 Secure the skirt with a small piece of tape or pretty label, or with a dot of glue. Cut a piece of ribbon approximately 6in. (15cm) long and tie around to hold the skirt in place like a sash; finish into a bow either in front or behind the skirt.

7 Cut a section of chenille stick approximately 6in. (15cm) long and bend in half; bend around the last bit at each end to make little hands and secure the sharp wire edges. Place the loop of the chenille stick behind the neck of the doll pin and glue in place. Bend and shape as desired to create arms.

8 Tuck a sprig of millinery flowers into the doll pin's arms. Add a small gem to one side of the head as a faux hair barrette, or add to the bodice as jewelry.

STEP 5

STEP 6

STEP 7

TINKER TIPS Complete steps 1–3 to a handful of doll pins to make many dolls at once, and then dress each one individually.

The simpler you keep your dolls' facial features, the easier they will be to mark.

Use smaller cupcake liners over regular sized liners to create peplums or bustles on dresses or fold up a liner at the neckline to make a high collar.

FANCY THIS Use the same liners for Clothespin Dolls and to create cupcakes for a cohesive party theme.

spool sprites

Empty thread spools become enchanted when outfitted with fairy wands and wings. Whether propped atop a cupcake, hidden between fronds in a potted plant, or secretly placed to surprise a special someone, these petite pixies are a cinch to make. But as with any spell, be warned—these Spool Sprites may steal your heart in return for wishes granted.

MATERIALS

Wooden spools

Sequins

Tooth picks (cocktail sticks)

Small cupcake liners

Chenille stick (pipe cleaner)

Cotton ball or skein of embroidery floss

TOOLS

Clear nail polish

Fine-point permanent markers

Craft glue

Scissors

1 Apply a light coat of clear nail polish to a section of the upper spool—this will be where you draw a face. The nail polish will prevent the ink from bleeding into the wood grain when you draw the face. Allow to dry.

2 Practice how you will draw a face on paper first. When you are ready, draw the face onto the spool with permanent markers. Using craft glue, stick a sequin close to one end of a toothpick and allow to dry—this will be the wand.

3 Trim off the circular base of a small, decorative cupcake liner, so that the sides make a long strip of paper, and wrap this around the spool to form a skirt. Secure in place with a dab of glue.

4 Cut a section of chenille stick approximately 6in. (15cm) long, then bend it around the spool as arms, securing at the back of the spool with craft glue. Bend the tip of each end into a small loop to serve as hands; place the wand into one "hand" and bend as required so it is grasped tightly.

STEP 2

STEP 4

TINKER TIP Read all directions before you begin because steps 1–3 require time to dry.

5 For the hair, cut at least 12 strands of embroidery floss about 6in. (15cm) long. Bundle and tie together using one strand—the knot becomes where the hair parts. You could pull a few strands from each side together at the front and trim as bangs (fringe).

6 Glue the hair to the top of the spool and let dry. Alternatively, glue a cotton ball to the top of the spool and shape and trim into a hairstyle.

7 For a crown, flatten a cupcake liner and fold around your index finger, adjusting until you have a cone. Secure with glue and trim off the tip of the cone to fit your sprite's hair; stick on with craft glue.

8 For wings, flatten another cupcake liner, fold in half and then again into quarters. Round off the corners at the top edge and then unfold—you should have a four-petal flower shape.

9 Cut the flower shape into four petal-shape wings. Secure a pair of wings to the back of each Spool Sprite using a dab of craft glue and hold in place until dry.

TINKER TIPS Complete steps 1–3 with a handful of emptied spools to make many Spool Sprites at once.

If using the Spool Sprite on a frosted cupcake, prop atop a thin wooden dowel to keep it clean; keep away from flames.

FANCY THIS Hang sprites from high places with clear or fine thread to make them look like they are flying.

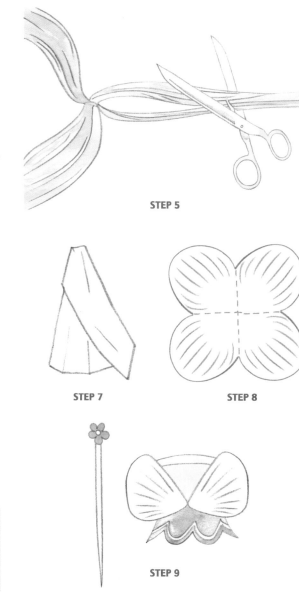

STEP 5

STEP 7

STEP 8

STEP 9

craft-stick frames

What better way to show affection for the simpler things in life than with a trio of frames cobbled from craft sticks? Odd scraps of fabric showcased in squares of wood and hung from ribbon are sure to bring an unpretentious charm to any space where prettiness prevails. Think of this craft as quilting for non-sewers. Add as many frames as you wish to suit the space you have.

MATERIALS
4 craft sticks per frame
Heavy plain paper or
card stock
Fabric
40in. (100cm) ribbon
Paper roses, gems, or
tiny seashells

TOOLS
Craft glue
Paint, latex or craft
Foam brush
Scissors
Glue stick
Tape
Wax paper to protect
work surface

1 On a protected work surface, create a square frame using four craft sticks. Secure with dots of craft glue at each corner. Make your squares—I made three in all—and allow to dry. For a slightly weathered appearance, use a dry foam brush to apply a light coat of paint to the front of each square; let dry.

2 Trim a piece of paper or card stock to fit the back of each frame. Set aside. Place the frames over the fabric to decide what area of pattern to showcase. Use the paper or card stock squares as templates to cut a piece of fabric to fit each frame.

3 Lightly cover one side of each piece of paper or card stock with an even layer of glue-stick adhesive, and then smooth on the fabric. Make sure the fabric is flat and aligned correctly and then trim any excess at the edges. Once your sturdy squares are covered with fabric, they are ready to be framed.

4 To frame your square of fabric, draw a fine line of craft glue along the perimeter edges of the first square and gently place the frame on top. Adjust as needed, press lightly to secure, and allow to dry thoroughly. Repeat for the remaining frames.

STEP 1

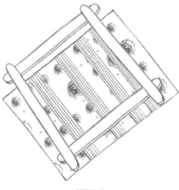

STEP 4

5 Fold the ribbon in half to form a loop for hanging. Lay all the frames down in a row face downward and place the ribbon on top with each strand flat. Secure temporarily by taping across the ribbon at the top of each frame. Hang the frames to check positioning and make any adjustments needed.

6 To finish, add more tape, if necessary, to fix the frames more securely in place, or stick the frames permanently to the ribbon with dabs of craft glue. Add a paper rose, a gem, or a seashell to the top of each frame.

STEP 5

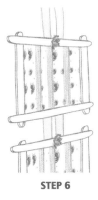

STEP 6

TINKER TIP Less glue and light paint means shorter drying time, resulting in a project that is ready for display not long after completion.

FANCY THIS For a twist on this project, shift frames to hang in a pattern of diamonds. For added whimsy, paint each frame or even each stick a different color, sticking to a faded palette that complements each fabric.

chapter 2
tinkering supplies

Remnants from home building, office supply stores, and even the baking aisle don't need to be plain to remain dutiful. Add a bit of flair to even the smallest of items and you will have charm to spare in any space. In this section, we'll tinker things such as ceramic tiles, shipping tags, and even toothpicks (cocktail sticks). You'll begin to give a second glance to everything that surrounds you and know that anything practical can be pretty, too.

tinkered tiles

Add pattern and print to any space when you decorate standard ceramic tiles to scatter about. Intended to line bath and kitchen walls, these are readily available at home improvement stores for little cost. Bestow warmth and whimsy to these cool squares with a treatment of paper and decoupage, and use instead to work triple duty around the home as paperweights, coasters, and trivets.

MATERIALS
Plain white ceramic
wall tiles
Pretty paper (*see page 16*)

TOOLS
Pencil
Sharp scissors
Decoupage medium
Small foam brush
Blow dryer, optional
Wax paper to protect
work surface

FANCY THIS Setting a motif off-center will add interest to your design. Try using a small, centered image instead of covering the entire tile with pretty paper (*see Desk Tidy project on page 60*).

1 Take a tile and begin by making sure it is clean and dry. Trace around the tile onto the selected paper and cut out a piece to cover the entire top surface.

2 Lightly brush or stipple (make small dots) decoupage medium to the back of the paper and gently position onto the tile, smoothing flat. Brush a light coat of decoupage medium over the entire top surface for a consistent finish.

3 Smooth any wrinkles either after a few minutes, or immediately using direct heat from a blow dryer. Let the first coat dry and then continue to add single coats of decoupage medium, allowing to dry completely between coats, until you have the finish you want.

4 If you will be using the tiles as drink coasters, apply quite a few coats of decoupage medium to waterproof the top surface and protect from stains.

5 Repeat with more tiles.

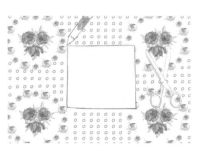

STEP 1

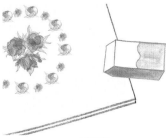

STEP 2

STEP 3

pretty tags

Whether white or manila, scalloped or geometric, shipping tags need little more than scraps to become present-perfect. Enjoy adorning these miniature canvases with papers and gems. Replace the standard white string with baker's twine or embroidery floss for added flair.

MATERIALS

Plain paper tags

Pretty paper (*see page 16*) in two coordinating designs

Baker's twine, embroidery floss, or narrow ribbon

Paper roses, gems, sequins, trimmings, applique, or buttons (optional)

TOOLS

Glue stick

Scissors

Pencil

Hole punch

Decorative paper punch (optional)

FANCY THIS Bind a length of ribbon to a tag and secure with a corsage pin to display or gift favorite trimmings. Be sure to cover the sharp tip of the pin with a scrap of pretty label.

If desired, add further decoration to each tag, such as a paper rose, small gems, sequins, or a pretty button.

1 Begin by removing the string from the tag. Use the glue stick to apply a light coating of adhesive to one side of the tag, and then press it to the reverse of a scrap of slightly larger pretty paper. Carefully trim off excess paper around the edges of the tag until you have a paper-covered tag.

2 Use a pencil to feel and mark the position of the original hole in the tag and punch a new hole to match through the paper covering.

3 Use the decorative hole punch to cut a circle or other shape from the contrasting pretty paper as an embellishment, and stick to the front of the tag. Add trimmings as desired.

4 Fold a length of baker's twine, floss, or narrow ribbon in half, thread the loop through the hole in the tag, and then pull the ends through the loop. Your tag is now ready for hanging.

STEP 1

STEP 2

STEP 3

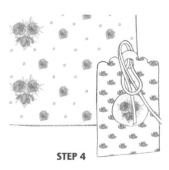

STEP 4

magnetic petits fours

Chunky magnets will easily resemble dainty miniature cakes when iced with printed paper and dotted with paper roses. Follow the simple step of placing pretty paper on the adhesive foam of each square and trimming to fit. As strong as they are pretty, you will enjoy putting these petals to the metal.

MATERIALS
Foam-backed adhesive magnets
Pretty paper (*see page 16*)
Paper roses, large gems, or decorative buttons

TOOLS
Pencil
Scissors
Craft glue

FANCY THIS Be tray-chic by hanging a metal platter as a memo board to display sentimental notes. Or keep magnets within reach nested in the papers of a fancy candy box.

1 Foam-backed adhesive magnets are generally packaged in semi-perforated rows of three, so break the magnets apart into separate squares. Either cut random squares of pretty paper to cover each magnet, or use one magnet square as a pattern and trace around it onto the paper.

2 Peel off the protective backing on one magnet to reveal the sticky foam top—note that the adhesive is quite strong, so you will need to get the positioning right first time. Place a small square of pretty paper face-up over the top and press down gently to secure.

3 Flip the magnet over and trim any excess paper as close to the edges of the square as possible. Repeat Steps 2 and 3 to create as many paper-covered magnets as you would like.

4 Top the patterned magnet square with a paper rose, secured with a dab of craft glue, to resemble a petit four. Alternatively you could stick on a large gem or a decorative button.

STEP 1

STEP 2

STEP 3

STEP 4

cupcake flags & bunting

Signal that any day is a special occasion by festooning everything with little pennants! Cupcakes, muffins, and even sandwiches are elevated to epicurean levels when a bit of frippery is added. Snips of paper diamonds folded in two become no-sew flags when secured to tooth picks or strung along string. Create on a larger scale to trim a room in a carnival of delightful prints.

MATERIALS

Construction paper
Pretty paper (*see page 16*)
Tooth picks (cocktail sticks)
String, embroidery floss, or narrow ribbon
Gems or paper roses (optional)

TOOLS

Scissors
Pencil
Ruler
Pattern-edge scissors or pinking shears
Glue stick
Wax paper to protect work surface

1 To create a template, fold a piece of construction paper in half, making sure to crease well. Cut a triangle shape down from the fold; when opened you should have a diamond shape. Make a small flag template for cupcake flags; make a large flag template for bunting (with the finished triangle about 4in./10cm long from fold to tip).

2 Fold a piece of the pretty paper in half and crease well. Slip your template over the fold and then trace around the triangle with a pencil. Cut out the shape. Repeat until you have as many cupcake or bunting flags as you need.

3 On the larger bunting triangles, try using pattern-edge scissors or pinking shears when cutting the sides to create added interest.

4 Open each of the flags out into a diamond shape and lay flat on the wax paper, decorative side downward. Apply a light coat of adhesive to the back of each diamond with the glue stick, making sure to cover right up to the edges.

5 For the cupcake flags slip one end of a toothpick along the inner fold, positioning it so the flag will sit toward the top.

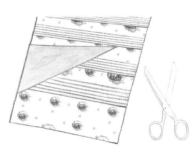

STEP 2

STEP 3

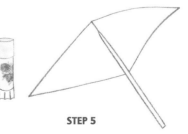

STEP 5

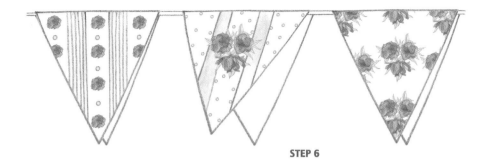

STEP 6

6 For bunting, lay the string, embroidery floss, or narrow ribbon along the inner fold of each flag, spacing the flags a little way apart. Close the "diamond" along the tooth pick or string, making sure to align the cut edges.

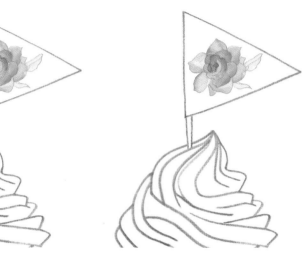

7 Press each flag firmly to smooth as needed and allow to dry completely. You can leave each flag as-is or decorate it with gems or paper roses. Hang up the bunting and add each cupcake flag to the top of a cake.

STEP 7

TINKER TIPS To put a unique spin on flags for parties, use paper from menus, invitations, stationery, and more.

To personalize the cupcake flags, type a list of words toward the center of a document with plenty of space between each, and then print, fold and cut.

FANCY THIS Instead of toothpicks, close and glue small diamond cutouts along a strand of colorful string, then tie the ends to two paper straws to form a mini clothesline. Pitch into a large cake for a festive banner.

shabby cheep birdhouse

An unfinished wooden birdhouse makes for a fun little fixer-upper. Paint, paper, and a downpour of glitter combine to make a delightfully impractical abode that's too delicate for outdoors but ready to roost on a shelf or perch on a peg.

MATERIALS
Wooden birdhouse
Pretty paper or pretty labels
(*see page 16*)
White or crystal glitter
Strand of fused pearls
Millinery flowers, chenille
chick (optional)

TOOLS
Paint
Foam brush
Scissors
Glue stick
Pen or pencil
Decoupage medium
Paper plate as glitter tray
Craft glue
Wax paper to protect
work surface

TINKER TIP Try applying scraps to the roof like shingles, creating rows repeating shapes that overlap from bottom to top.

FANCY THIS Decorate a group of bird houses with sturdy perches and mount in a row to use as pegs for hanging lightweight items such as jewelry, dish towels, or kitchen tools.

1 Begin by painting your birdhouse—use any paint meant for wood, such as craft paint or latex, and apply using a dry foam brush. Cover all sides that will be visible, including the bottom if you plan to hang the birdhouse. Apply as many coats of paint as desired, although for a "shabby" feel, one coat is all you need. Allow to dry.

2 Gather your pretty paper and/or pretty labels—this is a perfect project for making use of odd scraps. Apply random scraps of paper using the glue stick—or use pretty labels—until the birdhouse is covered to your liking.

3 To cut the scraps to fit onto any special ornamentation, turn the birdhouse over and mark around the shape with a pen or pencil onto the back of the pretty paper. Cut away any excess paper along the marked line and then glue the shape in place.

4 Seal the paper with a light coat of decoupage medium. Allow to dry slightly and then gently smooth away any bumps. Let dry completely. Apply another light coat of decoupage medium anywhere you would like to add glitter. Sprinkle glitter to cover the decoupage medium before it dries, and then shake off any excess.

5 Trim a strand of fused pearls to fit any details, such as along the decorative trim at the front of the roof, and fix with a light line of craft glue; let dry. Depending on the style of your birdhouse, you may want to add additional embellishments, such as tucking a cluster of millinery flowers into flower boxes or perching a chenille chick into the cutout circle.

STEP 2

STEP 3

STEP 4

STEP 5

favor baskets

Visit your local paint seller and you will be greeted with a panorama of neatly displayed paint chips: the cards that show a range of related paint colors available from a manufacturer. As sturdy as they are colorful, these cards are perfect for folding, snipping, and taping into small favor baskets.

MATERIALS
Two paint chip strips
per basket
Pretty paper (*see page 16*)
Ribbon or trimming
Cabochons or gems

TOOLS
Marker or pen
Scissors
Clear tape or pretty label
Large paper punch
Glue stick
Craft glue
Wax paper to protect
work surface

1 Fold one three-color paint chip into thirds; use a marker or a pen as a folding tool to crease the folds well. Rotate the paint chip and fold into thirds the other way, again making hard creases using your pen.

2 Place the paint chip color-side down. Cut two slits in from each side, one along each crease to the point where it meets the first crease running the other way. This will total four slits.

3 Bend the sides of the middle section up, then bend the sides of the two outer sections up and toward each other to form a box. Secure the flaps discreetly with clear tape or use a pretty label.

4 Create a handle by trimming a narrow strip from a second paint chip. Secure one end inside the box with tape. Arc the strip over the box and secure on the other side.

5 Decorate the box with one of the following ideas: use a large decorative paper punch to cut a shape from pretty paper and fix with a light application of glue stick; glue a piece of trim or ribbon along the front; tie a piece of twine or ribbon around the center of the handle; add cabochons or gems.

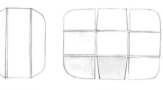

STEP 1   **STEP 2**

STEP 3

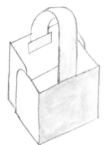
STEP 4

STEP 5

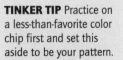
TINKER TIP Practice on a less-than-favorite color chip first and set this aside to be your pattern.
FANCY THIS Fill with small rocks or stones for use as decorative indoor balloon weights.

molded mirror

Available at home supply stores, lightweight plastic ceiling medallions (roses), designed to encircle a chandelier fixing, come in fanciful Victorian patterns and are paint-ready. Adorn a mirror with one of these molded disks and surround it in reflections with the shimmer of sparkling gems. Hang to brighten any space or use as a tray for perfume or jewelry.

MATERIALS
Molded plastic ceiling medallion
Paper doily
Mirror
Gems and mirrored findings

TOOLS
Craft paint (optional)
Foam brush
Scissors
Decoupage medium
Craft glue
Wax paper to protect work surface
Picture hanging hardware
Hot-glue gun and glue

FANCY THIS Decorate as described but use as intended for a one-of-a-kind ceiling medallion that is sure to add more than just architectural interest to any room.

1 Decide if you will paint the medallion or leave it white. Using a dry foam brush with craft paint, brush color onto the molded designs. To achieve a pale palette as shown opposite, use a very light touch when applying paint or allow painted areas to dry and then cover with a thin layer of white paint.

2 Find a paper doily approximately the size of the center of the medallion and trim away the plain inner circle. Brush decoupage medium to the reverse of the doily and press it firmly to the inner groove of the medallion. Make adjustments and fold and smooth as needed, then secure with a few light coats of decoupage medium.

3 Most craft stores sell round mirrors in a variety of sizes; find a size that is slightly larger than the center opening in the medallion. Draw a thin line of craft glue on the reverse of the medallion all around the opening; position over the mirror and press together to attach firmly. Allow to dry.

4 Decorate as desired by adding gems, such as pearly cabochons and mirrored findings. To hang the mirror, attach picture-hanging hardware to the top-reverse of the medallion, using a hot-glue gun.

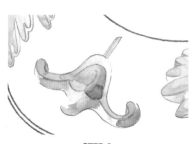

STEP 1

STEP 2

STEP 3

STEP 4

chapter 3
tinkering recyclables

You'll think twice about what gets placed in the recycling pile after
you see how quick and easy it is to tinker the ordinary, the practical,
and even the used into signature elements of cottage style. By simply
stopping to take notice of the imprinted flourishes on glass jars,
the regal ridges of bottle caps, or the sturdy shapes of tubes, you are
already on your way to creative recycling!

desk tidy

Ordinary cans find life after soup as extraordinary holders of supplies. Check your recycling bin and chances are that you have a vessel-in-waiting. Once treated to a shabby-style makeover, cans of all sizes become useful in any room. Use in the office to corral pens, pencils, and scissors; in the bathroom to hold makeup brushes; or in the kitchen for keeping wooden spoons at hand.

MATERIALS

Tin can
Image on paper
Glitter
Unused long eraser
Pretty paper (*see page 16*)
Short length of trim or braid
(optional)

TOOLS

Small hammer
Paint or spray paint
Foam brush
Scissors
Decoupage medium
Fine-point glue pen
Glue stick
Paper plates for decoupage,
paint palette, and glitter tray
Wax paper to protect
work surface

1 Prepare the cans by removing the labels and washing them very thoroughly. Allow the cans to dry completely both inside and out before proceeding, to avoid any rusting later, which would spoil your work. Carefully tap down any jagged edges at the open top of the can with a small hammer.

2 Paint the can using craft paint meant for metal, latex paint, or spray paint (but be prepared for the odd drip). Apply as many coats of paint as desired, allowing the can to dry thoroughly between each coat. Painting the bottom of the can is optional. I leave the inside unpainted.

3 Carefully trim out a suitable image from the background paper—I have used a flower motif from a sheet of pretty paper. Apply a light coat of decoupage medium to the reverse. Gently press the image to the side of the can, carefully smoothing out any bubbles or creases and making sure to press against any grooves in the can.

4 Brush over the entire image with a light coat of decoupage medium and let dry completely. Determine where you would like to add glitter and apply light, fine strokes with the glue pen (or a toothpick dipped in craft glue) to the desired area for the first glitter color.

STEP 3

STEP 4

5 Sprinkle glitter over the lines of glue. Shake off any excess glitter by gently tapping on the can. Allow the glue to dry completely. Repeat Steps 3 and 4 to add a second color of glitter, if desired. You can use as many colors of glitter as you like, but only add one at a time.

STEP 5

6 For the eraser, remove the card sleeve if it has one. Cut a narrow strip of pretty paper, fabric trim, or braid long enough to go right around the center of the eraser with a small overlap. Make sure the band is tight enough not to slip off easily, and then secure it in place with a dab of craft adhesive or a small piece of pretty label.

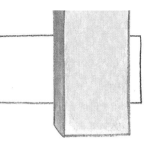

STEP 6

TINKER TIP To loosen stubborn labels from cans, submerge empty cans in warm, soapy water and leave them to soak thoroughly overnight.

FANCY THIS You can also decorate other stationery items to match for your desk tidy. To cover pencils, lay a pencil on a sheet of pretty paper and mark a rectangle the length of the pencil (excluding the eraser tip if there is one) and wide enough to wrap around the pencil with a slight overlap. Cut out the rectangle. Apply adhesive to the reverse of the rectangle using the glue stick, then carefully roll it around the pencil. Press in place firmly, smoothing out any wrinkles, and leave to dry. If the pencil does not have an eraser end, you can add a paper flower, ribbon bow, or a pennant *(see page 48)* to the end as further decoration.

To cover a pair of scissors, cut scraps from pretty labels and collage over the handles of the scissors until completely covered—but avoid covering the blades. Add several coats of decoupage medium to protect the surface, allowing each coat to dry thoroughly before applying the next.

Try adding a strip of pretty paper down the center of a ruler, being careful to avoid the measurement markings, or punch out a small circle of pretty paper to decorate the head of a tack pin.

If you don't want to use the can as a desk tidy, place a small tumbler filled with wildflowers inside instead for a vase that brims with rustic charm.

bottle-cap magnets

Give metal crown bottle caps the royal treatment by turning them into fetching holders of messages. Small circles of paper inserted and coated with dustings of glitter provide the magic necessary to galvanize these diamonds-in-the-rough into attractive sparklers destined to add a whimsical twist to any metal spot.

MATERIALS

Metal bottle caps, preferably twist-off type
Pretty paper (*see page 16*)
Crystal (white) glitter

TOOLS

Math compass
Scissors
Glue stick
Cotton swab
Decoupage medium
Adhesive-backed magnet strips
Paper plates for decoupage palette and glitter tray
Wax paper to protect work surface

FANCY THIS Instead of gluing the caps to magnets, look for bar pin backs in the jewelry-making section of a craft store and use to create brilliant one-of-a-kind brooches.

1 Lay the bottle cap flat with the crown pointing up. Determine what size the paper circle inserts will need to be to fit inside the cap, using a math compass. Set the compass to fit— approximately ½in. (1cm)—then, keeping it set, draw a light circle around a suitable motif on the pretty paper.

2 Using scissors, carefully cut out the circle of pretty paper and then use the glue stick to apply a light coat of adhesive to the reverse. Fix the circle to the base inside the bottle cap, smoothing it down firmly.

3 Dip a cotton swab into the decoupage medium and lightly swirl around the inside of the bottle cap and all over the image, to coat it completely. You may need to smooth the paper a bit as you go to remove wrinkles.

4 Follow immediately by sprinkling a generous amount of crystal glitter into the glue; shake off any excess glitter. Trim the magnetic strip to size and peel off the backing to affix it to the flat, reverse side of the bottle cap.

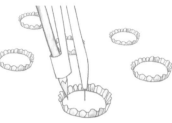

STEP 1

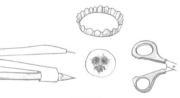

STEP 2

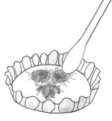

STEP 3

STEP 4

canning-jar pincushion

Mason jars—long prized for their durability, clean design, and tight-fitting lids—can easily be altered for uses other than food storage. Use to hold sewing notions and add a padded fabric pincushion to keep pins close at hand, or adorn flat lids with paper to showcase dry goods. Purchase a pack—they are cheaper by the dozen—and you'll have plenty to put to use in every room.

MATERIALS

Canning jar with 2-piece metal lid (flat lid and screw-on band)
Fabric
Cotton ball
Facial tissue
Pins
Thread spools or sewing notions (optional)
Pretty paper (see page 16)
Ribbon and millinery flowers

TOOLS

Paint
Foam brush
Scissors
Tape
Pencil
Glue stick
Decoupage medium
Paper plates for decoupage palette
Wax paper to protect work surface

1 Remove the 2-piece lid from the canning jar and paint the screw-on band using latex paint or craft paint meant for metal. Let dry completely.

2 Cut a circle of fabric an extra 1 in. (2.5cm) bigger in diameter than the flat section of the lid, and set aside. Gently pull apart a few cotton balls, place on the reverse of the lid, and form into a small mound.

3 Cover the mound with a paper tissue and test its thickness as a pincushion by inserting a pin; continue adding more cotton balls, if needed. Once the pad is thick enough to hold a pin, secure the tissue underneath the lid with tape.

STEP 1

STEP 2

STEP 3

4 Use the circle of fabric to cover the tissue, making small snips all along the rounded edge so it will fold over to the reverse neatly. Secure the edges underneath with tape. Fill the jar with sewing notions. Assemble the lid and screw onto the jar.

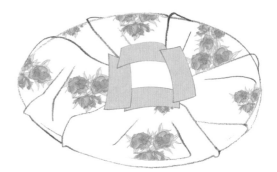

STEP 4

5 If you don't need a pincushion top, omit Steps 2-4 and follow Steps 5-6 to decoupage the lid instead. Use the flat lid to trace a circle onto the pretty paper. Cut out the marked circle, apply the glue stick to the reverse of the paper, and affix to the top of the lid, pressing firmly into place.

6 Apply a coat of decoupage medium to the paper and smooth out any bumps. Let dry and then fill the jar with colorful collections. Create a tasteful vignette by decorating canning jars of various sizes and displaying them together as a group.

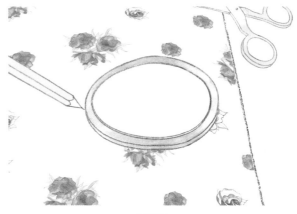

STEP 5

TINKER TIP Avoiding getting the decorated lids wet.

FANCY THIS Wrap jars with a band of ribbon and tie in a knot or bow. Tuck a sprig of millinery flowers close to the knot.

Tinker spools of thread for your pincushion jar by cutting squares of pretty labels, punching a hole in the center, sticking to the ends of a spool, and trimming to fit.

STEP 6

painted jars

A bit of paint and a few simple turns take ordinary jars from transparent to opaque. Simply pour, top, roll, and dry and a random assortment of jars and bottles suddenly becomes a unified set ready to adorn any room. Display the painted jars in clusters or along a shelf or windowsill for a shiny spectacle of soft hues. Fill with dry items such as paper flowers or cosmetic tools.

MATERIALS

Clean, dry empty glass jar, label removed, with lid
Pretty paper (*see page 16*)
Filler such as millinery flowers
Ribbon or trimming

TOOLS

Paint
Scissors
Glue stick
Craft glue
Wax paper to protect work surface

TINKER TIP Place a cupcake liner inside the base of the jar to protect any dry decorative fillers from the paint.

FANCY THIS For real impact, make several jars in the same color and display them as a group .

1 Pour the paint in your chosen color directly into the jar until it is just about one third full. Cover tightly with the lid.

2 Roll the jar about, even turn it upside down, until all the inside appears evenly covered with paint. Leave to dry for a few hours and then roll again. Remove the lid and allow any remaining paint to dry out thoroughly—this may take a day or two.

3 Cut a decoupage image or motif from your chosen paper and apply glue stick to the reverse. Fix to the best side of the jar.

4 Measure and cut a length of ribbon or trimming to fit neatly around the top of the jar. Apply a thin line of craft glue to the reverse of the ribbon or trimming and then secure around the top of the jar, holding firmly in place until it has set.

STEP 1

STEP 2

STEP 3

STEP 4

relish jars

Show your good taste by making use of emptied glass containers from jams, sauces, and mustards. This found-object-chic project calls for replacing labels and lavishly decorating lids to match. Refill with pretty provisions.

MATERIALS

Clean, dry empty glass jar, label removed, with screw-on lid

Pretty paper (*see page 16*)

TOOLS

Paint, optional
Foam brush
Ruler
Math compass
Scissors
Glue stick
Decoupage medium
Pinking shears
Paper plate for decoupage palette
Wax paper to protect work surface

1 Wash the jar and lid thoroughly. Stubborn labels or dried foods in grooves may require an overnight soak in warm, soapy water, followed by a gentle scraping. Let dry completely before moving on to the next step.

2 If choosing to paint the lid, use paint meant for metal, such as spray paint, latex, or multi-purpose craft paint, on the top and sides. Apply as many coats as desired, allowing to dry thoroughly between coats.

3 To decorate the lid with paper, measure the diameter of the lid just inside the top edge band and use a math compass to draw a circle that will fit on the pretty paper.

4 Cut the circle out and cover the reverse with adhesive using the glue stick. Fix the circle to the top of the lid and press down firmly. Seal the paper to the lid with a few coats of decoupage medium; allow to dry thoroughly between each coat.

5 Create a new label by measuring a smooth spot on the face of the jar and cutting a rectangle to fit with pinking shears. Decide where you will place the paper: either on the best face of the jar or over any original label or glue you could not remove.

6 Apply the glue stick to the back of the paper label and press securely onto the jar. Wipe away any smudges of glue. Do not seal with decoupage medium because it will make the glass look cloudy. Avoid getting labels or decorated lids wet.

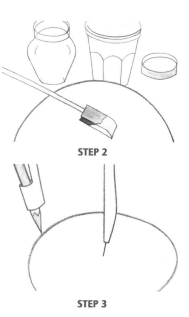

STEP 2

STEP 3

STEP 4

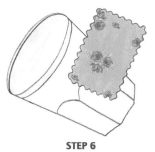

STEP 6

TINKER TIP To make a circle to fit using a math compass, place the point of the math compass at the center of the lid and adjust the arm to the inner groove. Carefully move the compass to a test sheet of construction paper, or directly to your selected paper, and lightly rotate to draw a circle.

FANCY THIS Create a set of jars to use in a craft room or an office and scrawl the contents of each jar either on the paper or on a shipping label layered over the decorative label.

hanging spice jars

Add a dash of sweetness to any space by reusing spice jars to hold diminutive blooms from the backyard. Gather violets, clovers, and buttercups or keep pinches of leafy herbs at the ready. Hang with twists of floral wire and arrange in multiples on pegs for a flavorful display.

MATERIALS

Clean, dry spice or other small jars with labels removed
Pretty paper (*see page 16*)
Floral wire
Fabric scraps
Appliqué, gems, or paper roses

TOOLS

Scissors
Glue stick

TINKER TIP For best results, avoid getting the labels wet.

If using outdoors, pass on adding the label and embellishments and hang the jars on branches for a delightful display.

FANCY THIS For added color, hang the jars with lengths of bright ribbon instead of using wire.

1 Begin by washing and drying the small jars thoroughly. Stubborn labels may require an overnight soak in warm soapy water, followed by a gentle scraping.

2 Trim a rectangle of pretty paper to fit the front face of jar. Coat the reverse of the paper with adhesive using the glue stick, and fix to the jar.

3 Take a length of floral wire around 30in. (75cm) long and fold it in half. At almost halfway, twist the two strands of wire to create a loop that will fit around the neck of the jar, below all the grooves.

4 Place the loop over the jar and twist the wire strands together on the other side to make a loop that can be tightened. Twist both ends close to the bottle until it is held securely in the wire.

5 Twist and knot the loose ends of wire together above the jar to create a hanging loop. Tuck any wire ends into the knot to secure. Tear a few strips from the fabric and tie them over the join to conceal the knot. Glue an appliqué, a rose, or a gem to the jar or vase to further decorate, if desired.

STEP 2

STEP 3

STEP 4

STEP 5

anytime crackers

This simple version of a Christmas cracker may not snap but is sure to add a pop of fun to even the smallest of gatherings. Collect small cardboard tubes to fill with keepsakes and then roll up in colorful paper napkins and tie with ribbon. Place at table settings for guests to pull open "wishbone style" to unleash a tiny shower of surprises.

MATERIALS

Cardboard or paper tubes
Plain white copy paper
Small prizes, candies,
or jewelry
Paper dinner napkin
Ribbon
Crepe paper
Pretty paper (*see page 16*)
Pretty labels

TOOLS

Scissors
Tape or craft glue
Pinking shears

FANCY THIS Create a celebration ensemble by decorating cracker fillers to match, using project scraps. Think small bundles wrapped and tied using the same napkins, papers, and ribbon.

1 Gather short cardboard tubes or cut longer ones to about 4in. (10cm) in length. Prior to decorating, provide each tube with a plain cover by trimming a band of white copy paper to fit and securing with tape or glue.

2 Open out a paper dinner napkin and lay down flat. Place the tube across one corner and roll the napkin up over it right across to the far corner. Secure the end corner of the napkin in place with tape.

3 Gather the loosely rolled napkin tightly together at one end of the tube and tie firmly with a length of ribbon. Fill each tube with the desired contents, then tie at the other end. Your tube should now resemble a wrapped candy. Trim off excess napkin with pinking shears, if desired.

4 Add layers to decorate your tube. First wrap a band of crepe paper around the center of the tube and tape or glue in place. Next, trim a length of pretty paper to layer over the band of crepe paper. Secure with tape or a piece of pretty label.

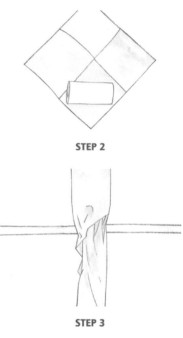

STEP 2

STEP 3

STEP 4

place holders

Party guests will delight in finding their place at the table with markers hatched from egg cartons, tiny clay pots, and craft sticks. Paint one pot per eggcup to accommodate friends by the dozen. Reuse, or offer as unusual party favors that are sure to be appreciated.

MATERIALS

Egg carton in paper, pulp, or recycled fiber
Mini clay pots
Craft sticks
Sprigs of faux flowers

TOOLS

Latex or craft paint
Foam brush
Spray paint
Permanent fine-point marker
Paper plate for a palette
Wax paper to protect work surface

TINKER TIP To achieve sufficient drying time, this project will likely require a prep day and a make day.

FANCY THIS For a natural display that's garden-party-ready, skip all the painting and fill the pots with tiny blooms in soil instead. Label with a craft stick to identify each plant.

1 Wipe the egg carton clean, break it into two and brush away any debris. Paint the cup base using either latex or craft paint with a dry foam brush, or spray paint (the quicker route). It may take a few coats to get the finish and coverage you want. Allow for a sufficient amount of drying time—possibly overnight.

2 Next, paint the clay pots; spray paint gives the best coverage in the least amount of coats. In the project shown, pots were given 2 coats of spray paint followed by a brushed band of latex at the rim.

3 Finally, snap craft sticks in half and treat them to a light coat of white craft paint on each side. You will need half the amount of sticks as pots (6 pots need 3 sticks). Once the sticks are dry, write a number at the tip of each using a fine-point permanent marker.

4 Take some fabric flowers with stems and twist the stems into a bunch. Fold the bunched stems around into a ball that will fit into the bottom of the pot. Push the bunch into the pot and adjust until the flowers rest as you desire.

5 Once all the flowers are placed in the pots, stick a craft stick in each and adjust around the stems until each stick stands up straight. Place the pots in the cups of the egg carton.

STEP 1

STEP 2

STEP 4

party-favor cups

Host a few celebrations and, before long, stacks of assorted cups have materialized. Do yourself a favor and revamp cups from motley to matching using favorite prints, an easy-to-make template, and bits of trimming. Fill with treats for a get-together destined to be a classic.

MATERIALS
Party cup
Colored construction paper
Plain white copy paper
Pretty paper (*see page 16*)
Ribbon or trimming

TOOLS
Pencil
Scissors
Glue stick
Craft glue
Clip

TINKER TIP For a drinking version of this project, omit the ribbon or trimming at the top and consider sipping from colorful straws.

FANCY THIS Coordinate the cups with the Party-favor Bags (*see page 82*) and Pretty Tags (*see page 45*) for a sweet theme that you won't be able to find at any store.

1 Start by creating a template; carefully take apart one paper cup and discard the bottom. Flatten the cup and trace along the outside over colored construction paper to create a template.

2 Use your template to cut 2 sheets per cup: a first layer of white copy paper to conceal the original design and a top layer from pretty paper.

3 Wrap the cut white piece over the cup and fix in place, dabbing with the glue stick. Tip the cup upside-down and pat the paper down to get it as close to the lip as possible.

4 Apply the glue stick to the back of the piece cut from pretty paper and fix to the cup in the same way. Trim any excess paper at the bottom or cut small slits on any overhang and push to fit under the cup. Secure using craft glue.

5 Cut a length of ribbon or trimming to decorate around the top of the cup and secure in place with a thin line of craft glue. Hold this in place with a clip until dry. Finally, fill the decorated cup with treats!

6 Make coordinating forks to eat your treats by wrapping the base of the fork handle with a small strip of the same paper used to cover the cups.

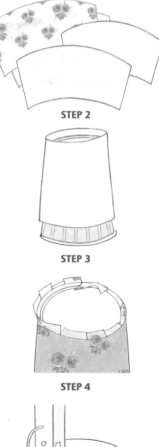

STEP 2

STEP 3

STEP 4

STEP 5

party-favor bags

A flat bottom makes paper lunch bags ready to stand and deliver, but if you add layers of folded liners, you'll have fanciful satchels ready to package favors and gifts, or smartly hold treats. No matter the occasion, raid the pantry for paper bags, cupcake liners, wallpaper scraps, and a bit of ribbon, and you'll be ever-ready to gift treats of any kind.

MATERIALS

Paper lunch bag with
a flat bottom
Pretty paper (*see page 16*)
Cupcake liners in 2 sizes
Brad (paper fastener),
beribboned tag, or ribbon
Length of wallpaper border
Narrow ribbon

TOOLS

Scissors
Decorative paper punch
Pattern-edge scissors
Clothespin or clip
Hole punch

1 Open a paper lunch bag so that it stands tall and fill with the desired contents. Fold the top over once and crease well. Cut a small circle from pretty paper with a decorative paper punch or pattern-edge scissors.

2 Take the circle of pretty paper and two different cupcake liners and fold in half separately, creasing well. Layer the folded papers and center them up, giving them another crease together.

3 Slip the creased papers over your folded bag top. You may want to secure them temporarily with a clothespin or clip. Punch a single hole through bag and liners at the center, just below the top of the lunch bag.

4 Run a brad or beribboned tag through the hole. Alternatively, you could punch two holes through bag and liners and string a piece of ribbon in and out, then tie at the front in a bow.

STEP 1

STEP 3

STEP 4

5 For a quick and simple version, cut a piece about 4in. (10cm) long from a roll of wallpaper border with a fairly small repeating motif, and fold in half to get a motif on each side.

6 Place the folded strip over the folded bag top and punch two holes through all layers, about 1in. (2.5cm) apart.

7 Thread the ends of a length of ribbon through the holes from front to back and pull tight. Even up the two ends of ribbon at the back.

8 Then thread the right-hand ribbon end back through the left-hand hole and vice versa, so both ends are now on the front. Pull both ends tight to secure. Trim to even the ends, if necessary.

STEP 6

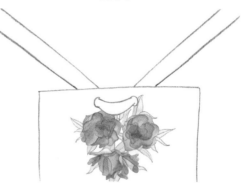

STEP 7

STEP 8

TINKER TIP Combine lacy circular doilies with pastel cupcake liners, and use a millinery flower to hold the bag closed, for a party favor bag with oodles of pretty feminine charm.

Coordinate the party favor bags with other party paperware—see Party-favor Cups on page 80.

FANCY THIS For contents that coordinate, showcase assorted goodies in clear plastic sandwich bags, then decorate by slipping a length of folded pretty paper over the top and stapling shut.

treasure tin

Allow emptied tins to show their mettle by remaking them into sturdy contraptions for business cards or handy catchalls for small supplies. Keep hinged lids flipped open to display, or shut tight to keep the contents in mint condition.

MATERIALS
Clean mints tin
Pretty paper (*see page 16*)

TOOLS
Latex or spray paint
Foam brush
Ruler
Scissors
Glue stick
Decoupage medium
Paper plate for decoupage palette
Wax paper to protect work surface

FANCY THIS Use treasure tins for small sewing kits, to hold change and tokens, or make in multitudes to serve as personalized party favors.

1 Begin by washing away any debris left from the mints and then allow the tin to dry well prior to painting. If you want more of a rustic feel, opt for latex and apply with a dry foam brush; for a more even coat inside and out, use spray paint.

2 Apply as many coats of paint as needed to achieve the look you like best. If you do not intend to keep the tin open, painting the inside is optional. Let the tin dry completely and then measure and trim a rectangle of pretty paper to cover the top-center of the lid.

3 You may also cut thin strips to decorate the sides of the tin—just make sure these do not hinder the opening and closing of the tin. Fix the paper in place using the glue stick and then seal all the decoration on the outside with one to three coats of decoupage medium.

4 If decorating the inside of the tin, measure and trim a rectangle of pretty paper to cover the inside as desired—perhaps just the bottom of the base and inside the lid, or the sides. Fix the paper using the glue stick and then seal with one to three coats of decoupage medium. Allow to dry completely before adding the contents.

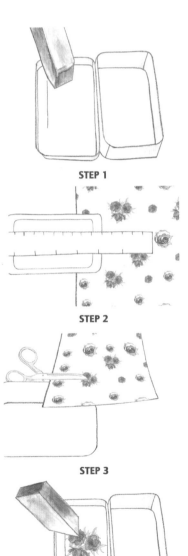

STEP 1

STEP 2

STEP 3

STEP 4

mint-tin shadow box

A mint tin makes a perfect stage for a petite ballerina in pirouette. With fused beading standing in for vanity lights and a mirror created by punching through paper layered over the shiny metal, your diorama is as portable as it is dainty and ready for performances at home or on the road.

MATERIALS
Mint tin
Pretty paper (*see page 16*) or paint chip
Ballerina cupcake topper or small toy
Fused pearls
Glittered dimensional scrapbooking stickers

TOOLS
Pen
Scissors
Glue stick
1-in. (2.5-cm) circular decorative paper punch
Craft glue
Wax paper to protect work surface

TINKER TIP Find ballerina cupcake toppers at online retailers or old bakeries, or use tiny dolls, toys, or ornaments.

FANCY THIS Secure a ribbon to the back of your shadow box and hang alongside pink slippers and a tutu of tulle for a pretty tableau worthy of a prima ballerina.

1 Take an empty, clean, and dry mint tin and trace around it onto the wrong side of the pretty paper or paint chip. Cut out three shapes: one for the top, one for inside the lid and one for the inside base of the box. For the sides, measure strips of paper, avoiding the box hinges, and trim to fit.

2 To create a mirror for the ballerina, punch a 1-in. (2.5-cm) diameter circle from the center of the paper shape for the inside lid of the box. Cover the reverse of the paper with glue stick and stick down. Place a length of fused beads around the inside edge of the lid, trim to fit and then fix in place with a line of craft glue.

3 Use the other cut pieces of paper to line the remaining surfaces of the box. Fix the paper in place using the glue stick and let dry. Add the ballerina in front of the mirror with a dab of craft glue. Continue to decorate your shadow box using stickers or punched paper.

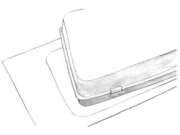

STEP 1

STEP 2

STEP 3

chapter 4
tinkering bits & bobs

Bits and bobs or odds and ends—whatever you call them, most of us have them: small piles of saved or collected remnants that seem to regenerate over time. In this section, scraps get put to great use in a myriad of projects. Discover how to combine things you already have in new and wonderful ways.

clothes hangers

Why should clothes have all the fun? Add some "beautility" (beauty + utility) to your closet by covering wire, wood, and even plastic hangers with fabric and paper. You can fashion enough for a wardrobe in no time, as they are so easy to create. They are perfect for holding special attire and lovely for displaying favorite frocks on hooks as wall décor.

MATERIALS

Wooden and wire hangers
Pretty paper (*see page 16*)
Patterned fabric
Buttons, fabric appliqué, or ribbon
Fabric
Construction paper

TOOLS

Painter's tape
Paint or spray paint
Foam brush
Decorative paper punch
Glue stick
Decoupage medium
Pinking shears
Craft glue
Paper plate for paint palette
Wax paper to protect work surface

1 Cover the base of the metal hook of a clean, dry wooden hanger with painter's tape, so paint will not spread up onto the metal.

2 Paint the hanger with either latex or craft paint using a dry foam brush, or spray paint. Apply as many coats as desired. Remove the painter's tape almost immediately and allow the hanger to dry.

3 Using a decorative paper punch, make shapes from pretty paper and fix to your hanger at random using the glue stick. Alternatively, completely cover the hanger with a collage of scraps of pretty paper. Seal the paper pieces with a few coats of decoupage medium.

4 Using pinking shears, cut a narrow strip of fabric long enough to tie in a bow at the neck of the metal hook.

5 Use craft glue to add buttons, fabric appliqués, ribbon, or other notions to your hanger, but avoid the arms of the hanger where they could interfere with clothing.

STEP 1

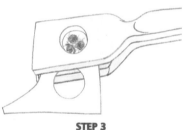

STEP 3

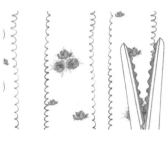

STEP 4

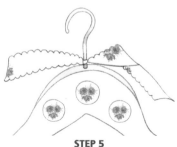

STEP 5

6 To decorate a wire or plastic hanger, cut long strips of fabric about 1in. (2.5cm) in width. Secure the end of the first strip to the tip of the hanger's hook with craft glue and a clip.

7 Begin to wrap the fabric taut in a downward spiral around the hanger. Start a new strip of fabric where the previous one finishes, securing the ends with another dab of glue. Continue until the hanger is covered. Make any adjustments by smoothing out creases or adding glue.

8 Alternatively, cut a full sheet of pretty paper to fit the triangular part of the hanger and fix in place with tape, then fold a second and third sheet around the arm on either side. Trim to fit as necessary and then secure using glue stick. Decorate the paper as desired with strips of trimming, or glue on decorative buttons or cabochons.

STEP 6

STEP 7

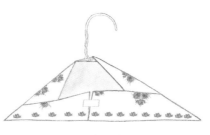

STEP 8

TINKER TIP Make a Pretty Tag (*see page 44*) using printed text like "Favorite Dress" or "For Baby" to hang from the hanger's hook.

Use pinking shears to cut a patterned strip of fabric to tie at the neck and use craft glue to add buttons, fabric appliqués, and other pretty notions to your hanger.

Allow the hangers to dry completely before using.

FANCY THIS Use a hanger as wall décor to display a special item of clothing such as a prom dress, or a ballerina's tutu suspended with ribbon.

Present these hangers as a unique gift for a bride-to-be and her bridesmaids, to display and admire their gowns before the wedding day. Decorate small hangers to gift baby, child, or doll clothes.

paper lanterns & chains

Simple paper crafts get an air of sophistication when made using delicately patterned papers and finished with ribbon. Festoon rooms year-long with lanterns and chains to signal a home buoyant with playful personality.

MATERIALS

Pretty paper (*see page 16*)
Ribbon
Embroidery floss
Beads (optional)
Pretty label (optional)

TOOLS

Scissors
Craft glue
Glue stick or tape
Paper cutter, optional

1 For the lanterns, fold the pretty paper in half and crease well. Cut slits no more than 3in. (7.5 cm) long spaced evenly all along the length of the crease. Open the paper so that the slits are running vertically.

2 Glue a length of ribbon along the top and bottom of the paper, leaving a pinch of room at each end to allow the ends to overlap slightly when they meet. Determine a top and bottom of your lantern.

3 Hold the paper so that the slits are vertical and bend it around so that the side edges meet to form a lantern. Secure discreetly with a dab of glue stick or a piece of tape at the top, the bottom, and a spot or two in between.

4 Add a handle by securing the ends of a narrow strip of paper inside the top edge on either side of the lantern.

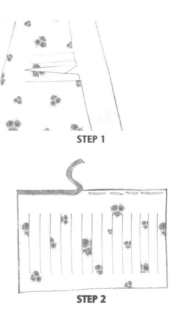

STEP 1

STEP 2

STEP 3

STEP 4

5 Alternatively cut a long piece of embroidery floss, fold in half and secure on each side to form a handle, allowing the ends to hang through longer than the lantern. Tie each end of floss in a bow or slip a bead through and double-knot to hold.

6 For paper chains, gather pretty paper in a mix of coordinating patterns—stripes, polka dots, and florals.

7 Cut the paper into equal strips approximately 6in. (15cm) long and 2in. (5cm) wide. Using a paper cutter makes this step a breeze due to ease and accuracy.

8 Bend the first strip into a loop and secure in place with tape or a piece of pretty label. Run a second strip of paper through the loop and then join and secure its ends. Continue until you have the desired chain length.

STEP 5

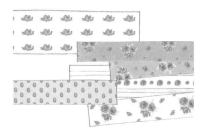

STEP 7

STEP 8

FANCY THIS Create delicate lacy lanterns by crafting them from paper doilies, first trimmed into squares or rectangles.

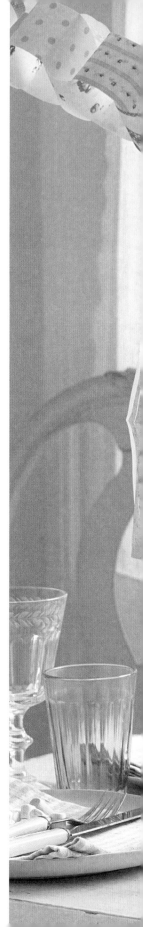

paper tussy mussies

Fold paper to fashion unfussy versions of Victorian tussy mussies. Because this adaptation uses paper instead of metal, fill with delicate goodies such as candies bundled and tied with twine, small bouquets of dried lavender, or even popcorn.

MATERIALS

Pretty paper (*see page 16*)
Embroidery floss
or ribbon lace
Paper roses, gems, beads

TOOLS

Pattern-edge scissors or
decorative-paper edge punch
Tape
Hole punch
Scissors

1 Start each project with a full sheet of pretty paper that is 8½ x 11 in. (21.5 x 27.9cm). Add extra detail by trimming the top and one side using pattern-edge scissors or a decorative paper edge punch.

2 For the packet: Positioning the paper with longer edges to the sides and with the decorated edge at the top, bend into a loop and secure with tape to form a barrel.

3 Gently flatten and then fold up the bottom undecorated end, securing with tape. Punch two holes a little below the top decorated edge on either side.

4 String a piece of embroidery floss or ribbon through and tie around each hole, leaving some slack between to serve as a handle.

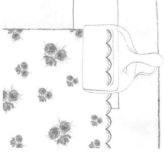

STEP 1

STEP 3

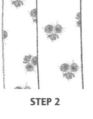

STEP 2

STEP 4

5 For the envelope: Positioning the paper with longer edges to the sides and with the decorated edge at the top, bend into a loop and secure with tape to form a barrel. Gently flatten the barrel. Fold up the bottom edge, folding the two corners in, and tape in place.

6 Fold over the top third to form a flap. String a piece of embroidery floss along the crease if you want the envelope to hang.

7 For the cone: Positioning the paper with longer edges to the sides, fold the paper in half and then cut a curve down one side.

8 Cut a decorated edge along the top. Bend the shape into a funnel, adjusting until the top is wide and the bottom is closed. Secure with tape.

9 Punch two holes a little below the top edge and string a piece of lace through for hanging. Embellish the tussie mussies as desired, with paper roses, gems, or beads.

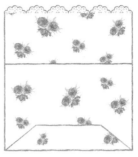

STEP 5

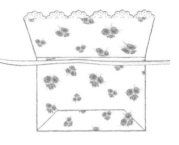

STEP 6

STEP 7

STEP 8

STEP 9

journal cover

Express yourself cover-to-cover with a plain journal turned dearest diary. Swathe a pad in a meadow of printed pastels, band with fabric, and tuck in a pencil to be ever ready to scribble down those inner treasured thoughts.

MATERIALS
Plain white copy paper
Journal or small book
1 or 2 sheets pretty paper
(*see page 16*) per book
Paper doily
Length of wide ribbon or
a strip of fabric
Pencil

TOOLS
Tape, Washi, or decorative
tape (optional)
Glue stick
Scissors
Pen for making creases

TINKER TIP If two sheets of paper are needed, attach them together on the left side with a band of decorated tape such as Washi, available in paper, fabric, or tissue.

FANCY THIS Cover a stack of books, tie together with a length of ribbon, and place on an old chair for a vintage-Romantic display.

1 Lay out the copy paper with the shorter edges to the sides. Place the journal on the right-hand half of the paper and determine if one sheet will be enough to fold and cover the book with extra paper (about 2in/5cm) on each side. If another sheet is required, simply tape to the first sheet to get the area needed. Gently fold the paper around the journal.

2 Remove the journal. Cover one side of the copy paper with adhesive using the glue stick and stick on a layer of pretty paper. Put the cover back on the journal and double check that the existing folds made in Step 1 work neatly—if they do not, re-fold.

3 Remove the journal again and crease all the folds well so they are crisp and sharp. Put the finished cover back onto the journal. Decorate the cover further, if desired, by sticking on a doily, paper flowers, or a motif cut from coordinating pretty paper.

4 Band around the outside with a piece of wide ribbon or torn fabric to keep the journal closed, tying in a bow or knot to secure. Tuck a pencil into the band.

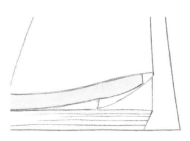

STEP 1

STEP 2

STEP 3

STEP 4

bookmarks

Save your page in style with this novel idea that fashions bookmarks from strips of sturdy card stock. A strand for a tassel, coupled with decorative edging, add finishing touches sure to hold interest from start to finish.

MATERIALS

Cardstock or paint chip strips
Pretty paper (*see page 16*)
Embroidery floss, ribbon, or baker's twine

TOOLS

Glue stick
Scissors
Paper cutter, optional
Hole punch
Paper edge punch or pattern-edge scissors
Decorative paper punch

1 If using plain cardstock, cover one side with pretty paper, securing with the glue stick. Trim off any excess paper along the edges. Cut the cardstock and/or paint chips into strips of about 2 x 6in. (5 x 15cm). Using a paper cutter can add ease and accuracy to this step.

2 Punch a hole about ½in. (1cm) from the top of each strip. Create a tassel by folding a strand of embroidery floss, ribbon, or twine in half, pulling the loop through the hole and then pulling the ends through the loop to secure.

3 Trim the bottom and/or top edge of the bookmark using a paper edge punch or pattern-edge scissors to add extra detail. Decorate the front of the bookmark with punched paper strips or a punched motif fixed with a dab from the glue stick. Trim the edges to fit, if necessary.

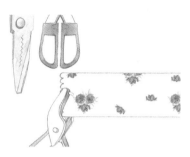

STEP 1

STEP 2

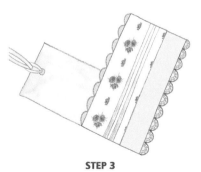

STEP 3

FANCY THIS Make bookmarks by the bunch and display in a painted can (*see the Desk Tidy on page 60*) as a reader's bouquet to keep at your favorite nook.

Use greeting cards and invitations instead of cardstock or paint chips, to coordinate with special occasions or to gift as small presents.

fabric-scrap garland

Make clever use of fabric scraps by tying them into a fluffy garland. Any scrap from your stash will suffice in this no-sew notion, which lends fanciful flair to any space. Hang to garnish rooms or soften mantles or doorways.

MATERIALS
Sturdy ribbon or binding
Assorted fabric scraps

TOOLS
Sharp scissors
Pinking shears

1 This project can be time consuming but is easy to pause and resume, take and make. Begin by cutting a piece of sturdy ribbon or binding the desired length of your garland; this will serve as the base. Be sure to allow some extra at each end (about 2in/5cm) for hanging when completed.

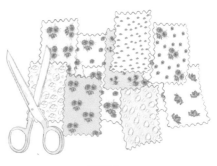

STEP 1

2 Using sharp scissors or pinking shears, cut lots of strips of assorted fabric. The strips can be long or short, narrow or wide, or all of the above! Experiment and play to see what will suit your style best. Tie each fabric strip tightly to the base, forming a knot.

STEP 2

3 Leave as little space as possible between each tied strip. Periodically, you may need to push the knots closer together to keep the garland nice and tight. Continue to tie and tie (and tie) until you feel your garland is complete.

TINKER TIP Cut many strips at once and then tie in stages to keep this project from becoming tiresome. Sit and tie while watching television, traveling, waiting...

FANCY THIS Add personality to your garland by using strips cut from favorite outworn clothing items, pieces of ribbon, shoelaces, ric rac, and more.

STEP 3

doily & cupcake bunting

Simple folds of ruffled cupcake liners and lacy doilies quickly become stylish accoutrements when folded, fastened, and strung along string. Use to add cheap frills to any occasion!

MATERIALS

Embroidery floss, ribbon, or twine

Cupcake liners

Paper doilies

Wired paper roses or decorative brads (paper fasteners)

TOOLS

Scissors

Clip or peg, optional

Small hole punch

FANCY THIS Use doilies and cupcake liners in other ways to pamper any party! Band canning jars with doilies and secure with twine for refreshing glasses, or attach sets to the tops of folded bags to hold party favors (see page 82).

1 Begin by cutting a long length of floss, ribbon, or twine however long you want the bunting to be—this will serve as the base. Remember to allow a little extra at each end for fixing.

2 Flatten and then fold a cupcake liner in half and crease it well. Fold a paper doily in half. Place the folded doily over the folded cupcake liner and center up. You can add another smaller doily on top if desired.

STEP 2

3 Slide the liner and doily set over your base, making sure the floss sits snugly in the crease. Use a clip or peg to hold the layers together and then punch a hole below the fold through all four layers of paper.

STEP 3

4 Secure the layers by stringing a wired paper rose through the hole and bending the wire over at the back to fasten. Alternatively, push the arms of a brad/paper fastener through the hole and open out at the back.

5 Continue to make as many pennants as you would like for your bunting—this number will vary based on the length of your garland and the space you prefer between each pennant. Be sure to keep the ends free for hanging.

STEP 4

jewelry boxes

Purchase even a few pieces of jewelry and before long you have leaning towers of mismatched cartons. Unite rigid parcels with soft colors, floral motifs, and a shower of glitter, for containers as valued as their contents.

MATERIALS

Cardboard jewelry boxes
Pretty paper (*see page 16*)
White/crystal glitter
Trimming

TOOLS

Paint (latex)
Foam brush
Glue stick
Decoupage medium
Scissors
Clips
Paper plate as a palette and glitter tray
Wax paper to protect work surface

1 Using a dry foam brush dipped in latex paint, paint the exterior of each box, covering all sides except the bottom, and allow to dry. Decorate the lid with pieces of pretty paper, either cut to fit or centered, and fix using the glue stick.

2 Apply a light coat of decoupage medium over entire top of lid. Smooth any creases carefully before it is completely dry.

3 Apply a second light coat of decoupage medium or glue stick to the top of the lid and cover with glitter. Shake off excess glitter over a paper plate. Check for any missed places and re-glue and glitter, if needed.

4 Cut a piece of trimming to fit all around the sides of the lid. To apply the trimming, smooth glue onto the reverse and press in place; hold with a few clips until dry.

TINKER TIP For best results apply paint with a dry brush to keep the cardboard of the box from wrinkling.

FANCY THIS For an exquisite display, stack boxes and tie with a wide ribbon.

STEP 1

STEP 3

STEP 4

paper-scrap picture frame

Any tinkerer worth their weight in gems saves almost every scrap. Put collected paper remnants to good use on a picture frame where a mis-match of patterns seamlessly coalesces into a charming collage. It's perfect for framing photographs of other one-of-a-kind treasures: your family and friends.

MATERIALS

Wooden picture frame
Scraps of pretty paper and pretty label (*see page 16*)

TOOLS

Scissors
Glue stick
Decoupage medium
Foam brush
Paper plate as a palette
Wax paper to protect work surface

1 Trim pieces of pretty paper and pretty labels and fix to the frame, using the glue stick for the paper. Begin with hard-to-cover areas such as corners, where you may want to stick and then trim the paper to fit.

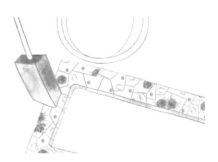

STEP 1

2 Continue to patch piece by piece all over the front of the frame—and along the sides, if you like. You may choose to follow a regular pattern of some kind or simply place pieces completely at random.

3 When the frame is covered as much as you like, apply a coat of decoupage medium all over the design and smooth any creases carefully. Let it dry completely. Apply more coats if desired, allowing to dry between each coat.

STEP 3

4 For added charm, rip a narrow strip of fabric and attach each end to the back of the frame with staples or tacks. Use to hang the frame.

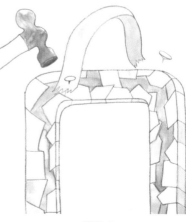

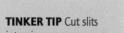
TINKER TIP Cut slits into pieces on corners so that they wrap easily on any curved sections of the frame.

STEP 4

embroidery-hoop mobile

Add romantic fairy style to any spot by converting the center ring of an embroidery hoop into an enchanting mobile of dangling ribbons. Simply cover the base by winding strips of fabric and suspend with a fastened trio of longer ribbons. Dot the outer band with paper roses to complete this almost-effortless endeavor that sweetly signals even the lightest of breezes.

MATERIALS

Fabric trimmed or torn into 1-in. (2.5-cm) strips
Embroidery hoop
Ribbon
Paper roses or gems

TOOLS

Scissors
Craft glue
Clip
Wax paper to protect work surface

TINKER TIP Pliable lightweight ribbon in a fairly narrow width is recommended for this project.

FANCY THIS Hang flat for a fanciful spin on a dream catcher.

1 Remove the outer ring of the embroidery hoop. Using craft glue, stick the end of the first strip of fabric to any spot on the inner ring and clamp in place to secure, until the glue is set.

2 Continue to wrap the ring tightly with the fabric strip, overlapping each layer slightly over the previous one. Start a new strip of fabric where the previous one ended, securing the ends with a dab of glue. Continue until the hoop is covered, then secure the end with another dab of craft glue and clip in place to dry.

3 Tie on three long lengths of ribbon so they are evenly spaced around the ring for hanging. Tie as many ribbons as you like to hang down from the ring. Fill empty spaces on the ring between ribbon knots with paper roses or other gems.

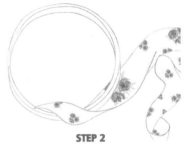

STEP 1

STEP 2

STEP 3

decoupage pots

Elevate inexpensive clay pots from drab to fab with a patchwork of prints using decoupage glue. Snip and tear fabric scraps into strips and squares and apply one by one until your pot is completely covered. The result is a soft mosaic that is anything but prosaic. Fill with small flowering plants for a lively windowsill vignette.

MATERIALS

Small terra cotta flowerpots

Fabric scraps

TOOLS

Cloth or paper towel

Decoupage medium

Foam brush

Paper plate for decoupage palette

Scissors

Wax paper to protect work surface

1 First remove any labels and wipe the surfaces of the clay pots with a cloth or paper towel. Have an assortment of cotton fabric scraps handy to snip and tear or cut into small squares and strips, until you have amassed a little pile.

2 Pour a medium-sized circle of decoupage medium onto a paper plate and dip a foam brush in; apply the decoupage medium onto the pot over small areas at a time and cover with fabric scraps.

3 Continue this process until the pot is completely covered on the outside and—if desired—on the inside, too. Allow to dry for a short period and then gently smooth away any frays or bumps. Leave the pot to dry completely.

4 Apply additional coats of decoupage medium to seal the fabric well, allowing to dry completely between coats. For best results, use these pots indoors only.

STEP 2

STEP 3

STEP 4

TINKER TIPS Cover the most time-consuming areas first, such as the bottom or top, then enjoy filling in the middle.

To cover overhangs at the top and bottom lips of the pot, snip a series of slits along the top of a strip of fabric, stick down the solid part first horizontally and then fold the slits over top and bottom and smooth flat.

FANCY THIS Save a larger square of fabric to tuck in each pot and use your shabby vessels to hold items such as sets of cutlery, for a table that's ready for impromptu, farm-fresh meals.

TINKER TIPS To reduce the risk of tears while smoothing wrinkles during the decoupage process, try using a barrier of wax paper between your fingers and the surface.

If using the pedestal to display food, line the saucer with a doily or flattened cupcake liner to protect the surface.

FANCY THIS Create Pot Pedestals at varying heights to display jewelry and trinkets on tiered levels.

pot pedestal

Take beautiful jewelry and trinkets to new levels by displaying them on a pedestal pieced from a clay flowerpot and a saucer. Unified neatly by a coat of paint, the mismatched parts become an elegant addition to any setting. A length of beaded trim from the bridal department adds glamour.

MATERIALS

Terra cotta flowerpot
Terra cotta saucer for a
pot twice the size of your pot
Pretty paper (*see page 16*)
Beaded trim

TOOLS

Cloth or paper towel
Paint, craft, latex or spray
Foam brush
Math compass
Scissors
Decoupage medium
Craft glue
Clip
Paper plate as palette
Wax paper to protect
work surface

1 Begin by selecting a pot and a saucer that sit level. Remove any labels and wipe surfaces with a cloth or a paper towel prior to painting. Apply coats of paint to the exterior of the pot and both sides of the saucer until you have the finish you like best.

2 Use a math compass to determine the size of circular paper insert that will be needed to fit inside the saucer. Draw the circle lightly onto the wrong side of the pretty paper and then cut it out. Apply a light coat of decoupage medium to the reverse of the circle, center onto the saucer and gently smooth out any creases.

3 Leave to dry, and then seal the circle with a few coats of decoupage medium allowing to dry completely between each coat. Using a heavy line of craft glue, secure the saucer to the base of the upside-down pot. Let dry completely.

4 Brush decoupage medium along the flat outer rim of the saucer and carefully cover with a length of beaded trim that has been cut to fit. Position and smooth as needed and clamp gently with a clip until dry and secure.

STEP 2

STEP 3

STEP 4

cookie tins

Freshly baked or purchased, no one will notice or care when cookies arrive packed in tins as tasteful as these. Round, white metal containers—available at craft stores and online—or emptied tins collecting in the cupboard readily take to fabric and ribbon, which makes decorating them easy as pie. Make a few to stack and a few to have handy for extra special gift-giving.

MATERIALS
Round, white metal tins
Fabric
Ribbon

TOOLS
Decoupage medium
Foam brush
Scissors
Construction paper
Paper plate as palette
Wax paper to protect
work surface

FANCY THIS Find tins in varying sizes to create a nested set of mix-and-match containers.

1 Remove any labels and wash and dry the tins prior to decorating. Place a piece of fabric over the lid to determine the placement of the pattern across the area.

2 Brush a light coat of decoupage medium across the lid and press the fabric in place. Trim the excess away around the edge of the lid. Apply a few light coats of decoupage medium to seal the fabric to the lid, smoothing any wrinkles, edges, and frays.

3 Brush decoupage medium along the sides of the tin below the area where the lid sits so as not to affect the functionality of the tin. Cut a length of ribbon to fit around the tin and stick in place with decoupage medium.

4 Smooth any frays where the two ends of the ribbon meet with a light stippling and brushing of the decoupage medium.

5 Trace around the lid onto construction paper to make a template; use this to cut out another circle from the fabric. Place the fabric circle inside the tin, leaving it loose so it can be washed or replaced easily.

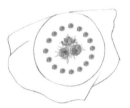

STEP 1

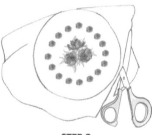

STEP 2

STEP 3

STEP 4

fabric-covered wreath

Spin a handful of materials into a cozy spot for two lovestruck feathered friends. A straw wreath and foam birds from the floral department easily combine with a craft stick and strips of fabric into a beautifully bucolic home accent destined to add a breath of springtime wherever it is displayed.

MATERIALS
Fabric
Straw wreath
2 foam and feather birds
Millinery flowers
Ribbon or trimming

TOOLS
Scissors
Craft glue
Craft stick

TINKER TIPS Any type of wreath or loop will do as your base, just be sure to add a perch that will fit; if a craft stick is too small, use a real branch.
    For best results, display the wreath indoors.

FANCY THIS For a different twist, after completing Step 2 tie short strips of fabric all around the wreath (*see the Fabric-scrap Garland on page 108*).

1 Trim or tear the fabric into strips about 1½in. (3cm) in width. Secure the end of a strip of fabric to any spot on the wreath with a dab of craft glue.

2 Continue to wrap the wreath tightly with the fabric strip, overlapping each layer slightly over the previous one. Start a new strip of fabric where the previous one ended, securing the ends with a dab of glue, until the wreath is completely covered.

3 Loop a fabric strip through the wreath for hanging. Make a perch by trimming or tearing a narrow length of fabric and wrapping it tightly around the craft stick from end to end. Secure the ends of the fabric with dabs of craft glue, clamping until dry, if needed.

4 Position the perch horizontally within the opening of the wreath towards the bottom, so that it fits across the wreath tightly; secure in place with further dabs of glue. Let dry until the perch is dry and stable.

5 Bend the wires at the base of each of the foam birds to position them to stand upright together on the perch. Tie a sprig of faux flowers to the wreath with a piece of ribbon or trimming.

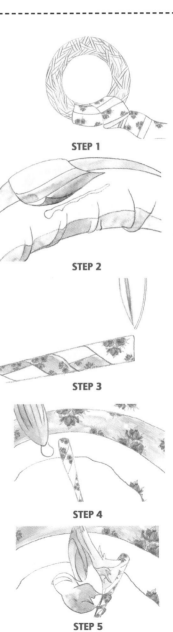

STEP 1

STEP 2

STEP 3

STEP 4

STEP 5

SUPPLIERS

Cath Kidston
Online retailer (USA) and stores (UK)
www.CathkidstonUSA.com
www.cathkidston.co.uk
Fabrics

Hobbycraft
Stores nationwide UK
www.hobbycraft.com
Arts and craft suppliers

Home Depot
Stores nationwide USA
www.HomeDepot.com
Ceramic tiles, spray paint, latex paint, paint chips, light switch covers

Ikea
Stores worldwide
www.Ikea.com
Scissors, construction paper, paper napkins, large white hangers

John Lewis
Stores nationwide UK and online retailer
www.johnlewis.com
Fabrics, stationery, kitchen supplies

Little Pink Studio
Online retailer
www.TheLittlePinkStudio.com
Vintage seam binding, rosebud appliques, ballerina cupcake toppers

MarthaStewart.com
Online retailer

www.MarthaStewart.com
Paper punches, fine glitter, fine-tip glue pens, cupcake liners, adhesive gems, craft paint

Michaels
Stores nationwide USA
www.Michaels.com
Arts and craft suppliers, unfinished wood items, stationery, cooking and sewing items, and much more

Shabby Fabrics
Online retailer
www.Shabbyfabrics.com
Wide range of pretty fabrics, including Lecien, available to view by color preference

Speckled Egg
Online retailer
www.Speckled-Egg.com
Vintage treasures and arty treats

Staples
Stores nationwide USA and UK
www.staples.com
Color copies, paper cutters, office tags, paper clips, mailing labels

Sugar Pink Boutique
Online retailer
www.sugarpinkboutique.com
Millinery flowers, berry beads, fat quarter bundles of fabric

The Shoppe At Somerset
Online retailer
www.stampington.com/shoppe
Baker's twine, decorated tape

Tinsel Trading
1 West 37th Street, New York, NY 10018. 212-730-1030
www.TinselTrading.com
German glass glitter

TJ Maxx
Stores nationwide USA
www.TJMaxx.com
Scrapbooking supplies

TK Maxx
Stores nationwide UK
www.TKMaxx.com
Scrapbooking supplies

Vintage Lizzie
Online retailer
www.vintagelizziestyle.blogspot.com
www.urbangardenstextiles.com
Fabrics featuring antique French roses

INDEX

ACKNOWLEDGMENTS

It is with much warmth and gratitude that I thank my fairy godmother, Fifi O'Neill, who responded quite magically to my "wish out loud" and guided me to CICO.

At CICO, I must begin with a heartfelt thank-you to Cindy Richards for finding my ideas "clever and lovely" and making my dream of a book come true; to Clare Sayer and Marie Clayton for their valued guidance; to photographer Holly Jolliffe and stylist Sophie Martell for showcasing my tinkerings in the most beautiful way; to designer Lucy Parissi for a lovely layout of dashed lines and scalloped boxes; to Qian Wu for rosy-patterned illustrations; and to Sally Powell for her help.

I thank my sisters Betsy and Dede for being cherished cheerleaders; my mom and dad for instilling confidence and passing along creativity; my family and dearest friends for their patience, laughs and treats; and my blogging friends for providing a sweet online clubhouse in which to share.

I owe everything to the unconditional love, support, and encouragement received every day from my husband and bestest friend Jeff, and our two amazing sons, Jonah and Ethan. All that I treasure in this world is possible because of you.